YAR

$1

D1102353

A Norfolk
Chronicle

The Author

A Norfolk Chronicle

Robert Bagshaw

Cover Illustration: Horsey Mill.
Photo: The Author.

By the Same Author:

Poppies To Paston.
Toothy Goes To War.
Norfolk Remembered.
More Memories of Norfolk.
Echoes of Old Norfolk

© Robert Bagshaw 1997
First published 1997

ISBN   Hardback: 0 900616 52 0
        Softback: 0 900616 53 9

        Printed and published by
        Geo. R. Reeve Ltd., 9-11 Town Green, Wymondham, Norfolk.

Contents

Illustrations

An Angler's Ode To Norfolk.

Green bowers that bend their glories to the brook,
Where, charmed with quiet content, I bait my hook;
Far from the world's tumultuous toil and strife,
I quaff the joyous elixir of life.
Nor envy no man while I yet may hear
The tuneful music of the rushing weir.

Oft by the rustic bridge at Mattishall
I've listened to the river's gentle fall,
And ever more its echoes back to me
Have borne the mystic voices of the sea.
Ah! Could those stones but utter half they've seen,
Oh, what a book of knowledge might have been.

And when the orb of day has passed the hill,
By Hockering Church, have we not paced the rill,
Started the sparrows from the growing corn,
Or played a game of bowls upon the lawn?
Or, after labour, idly sat at ease
And quaffed a measure at the old Cross Keys?

Within that famous hostel many a night
Have we not met, each other to delight;
Sung of John Barleycorn and pledged his health,
Ten fathoms deep, the source of England's wealth?
Their foreign wines and German beers are pale.
Give us our measure of the nut-brown ale.

Old and familiar friends so often met,
And hope to meet again; some sad regret
For those we loved who shall be found no more
To dance a frolic o'er the homely floor.
Let us then hold them dear while yet we may,
Burying unkindness with dead yesterday.

Fishing the Bure near Buxton.

To thee, dear Norfolk, till my soul forsake,
My thoughts must lead me, sleeping or awake;
A little moment from the world to steal,
And all the freedom of sweet Nature feel.
Dear homeland, my land, where is there a pen
Can half disclose thy grace to mortal men?

So for a little while, dear land, farewell.
Nor pen, nor tongue my love for thee can tell;
Exile has taught me in the crowded street
To seek thy peace wherein my end to meet.
Thy rural charms do far outvie for me
Ambition's greed or social vanity.

And this at least I ask of fickle fate,
To quit the turmoil ere it be too late;
But if too late, I fain would be interred
By some still pool the speckled trout hath stirred;
Where oft, with reel and line and tapering rod,
I've been alone and nearest unto God.

Norman Wrighton,
His Majesty's Theatre, London, S.W.
March 1st, 1913.

January 1st.

The Girl In Grey.

I wonder why the Norfolk of my childhood, when seen in retrospect, was continually bathed in pervasive and unbroken sunshine. At least, that is what my memory tells me, although I have no need to consult weather records of the twenties and early thirties to tell me it was not so.

I can recall the days when we sat in school wearing overcoats and gloves to keep out the cold - and then there was the occasional white Christmas. Even now, as that season approaches, my mind conjures up a Christmas Eve vision of North Walsham Market Place ankle-deep in snow, with the traders frantically reducing their prices in an effort to clear the festive produce from their stalls, and the Salvation Army Band gloriously spreading the message of Christ's birth. But those days were the exceptions. The real sunshine came from the happiness of our everyday lives, shielded as we were from the worries of the adult world.

There can be little doubt that modern children would consider our lives to have been dull in the extreme, but that was not so. Our world was a wonderland which we were free to enjoy more or less as we pleased. And happiness belongs to the unconscious, to be absorbed unawares. Children have very acute senses and they live a couple of feet or so nearer to the earth than do men and women. We smelt the daisies, the fragrant orchids and the clover as we went, without having to bend or pick. The miniature inhabitants of meadow and hayfield, the ants and spiders, the grasshoppers and caterpillars, were near, vivid and familiar. The summer grasses waved at eye-level and the beards of the barley tickled our cheeks. And it was against this sensuous background of summer days that my friend Jack and I absorbed our unconscious pleasure - and our happiness.

I think it could be said that we were "free range" lads, for Jack and I roamed at will over a wide radius around our home town. To one side there was Felmingham Heath and Westwick Woods; to the other Spa Common and Witton Woods. Our favourite territory, however, was on the banks of the Canal, formerly the

The banks of the River Ant, the focus of so many boyhood wanderings, 1928.

River Ant, upstream from Royston Bridge, and it was there that, when I was about ten years old, I had a strange encounter with two strangers. It was, furthermore, a brief encounter, so brief indeed that it would probably have become lost in the inner recesses of my memory if it had not been for the fact that, more than sixty years later and in unexpected circumstances, another encounter brought it vividly to the surface. But we must go back to the beginning.

Jack and I, alike in so many ways, were very different in one respect. As we lay on the canal bank, watching the changing cloud formations and anything else that caught our attention, he would always be quite happy to stay there all day. I, on the other hand, would become restless and feel the urge to be pressing on elsewhere. That was how it was that day.

"Dew yew go," he said. "I'll still be here when you get back".

So I set off, over the humpbacked bridge and along the dusty road in the direction of Bacton. It was a warm, sunny day in early summer, and I was a slow walker at times like that, for there was so much to see. There were birds' nests to be examined and their contents noted; there were voles and other hedgebank creatures rustling about among the dead leaves; and the first flowers of summer were pushing upwards in search of the welcome sun. In short, it seemed that the whole world of nature was awake and going about its business.

Eventually, a mile or so further on, I reached "The Farm House." We always called it that for, though it must have had a name, we had no knowledge of it. Nor did we know anything of its occupants, for it was a splendid house, with the farm spreading along the Bacton road and back towards Swafield, and, if there were any children, they certainly didn't come to the Council School. The house stood well back from the road and was approached by a long, circular drive which surrounded a vast lawn, in the middle of which stood a horse chestnut tree. And it was not just any old chestnut tree. Haughty and ancient, it thrust its branches upwards and outwards, throwing a canopy of shade over the entire lawn - certainly one of the most magnificent trees we had ever seen. In those days we knew nothing of class distinctions, but we regarded The Farm House as being somewhat out of our league.

Entrance to the drive from the road was by means of a five-barred gate, and it was as I reached this that I suddenly beheld a vision. There, in the shade of the tree, was a young girl, probably about eight years old, and she had obviously been watching my approach along the road. She smiled and waved, and my heart missed a beat as I waved back. Then she slowly came across the lawn towards me, and it was her appearance that made it such a strange encounter, for, in spite of the warmth of the day, she was clad in a thick grey overcoat with matching hat, and she even had mittens on her hands. What puzzled me even more, however, was the fact that her wrists, knees and neck were swathed in white bandages. I can only remember one sentence of our conversation:

"I'm unwell," she said.

I found this even more mystifying for, in our world, we were either well or we were ill. I had no comprehension of what had to happen to make somebody unwell.

Then, round the corner of the house came the figure of a man. I asked if he was her father.

"No," she replied. "He's my Uncle Jim."

Uncle Jim came over to join us.

"Hello," he said. "And who have we here?"

"I'm Bobbie Bagshaw," I replied.

"Oh," he said. "You must be Arthur Bagshaw's boy."

It did not surprise me to hear myself identified in that manner. My father was a journalist and, at that time, was covering that part of Norfolk for the *Eastern Daily Press*. It seemed quite natural to me that everybody should know him.

But then our brief encounter came to an end.

"Come along", said Uncle Jim to his niece. "It's chilly here in the shade, and you mustn't catch cold, you know." And then, turning to me, he added, "She's unwell."

With that, they were gone and I was left to my thoughts. For a while, the world of nature had lost its appeal, and I made my way back to the canal, where Jack was still lying on the bank, lost in a world of his own. I told him nothing of my encounter. It was something I wanted to keep to myself.

In the weeks that followed I went several times past the canal and up to the Farm House, hoping I might catch a glimpse of the little girl in grey, but I never did. Sometimes, as I rode to Bacton on my bicycle for a swim, I would catch a glimpse of Uncle Jim working in the fields and we would exchange waves, but that, it seemed, was the end of the story.

But it was not so. Many years were to pass – the greater part of a lifetime, in fact – and, having retired from the profession which had occupied most of my waking moments, I had gone back to my first love and settled down to writing. It was, in fact, one of my books that gave rise to an echo from the past when, in November, 1995, Jarrolds paid me the compliment of inviting me to speak at one of their Literary Luncheons. It was a very pleasant affair which concluded with a signing session, and it was during this that an elderly man presented himself before me with a request for my signature. He was Uncle Jim.

Needless to say, I cannot claim to have recognised him, for our previous meeting had been so brief and, indeed, so far back in the distant past. The mere mention of his name, however, instantly turned a forgotten memory into a vivid, crystal-clear reality. The only thing which defied my memory was the name of his young niece. I knew that it was not a name commonly used amongst my contemporaries – they were mostly Dorothys, Hildas and the like. I also knew that it was a name I associated with a book, but I had to wait for Uncle Jim to remind me. I really should have remembered the Book, for the little girl in grey was called Naomi.

With so many people around us, we were not able to continue

our conversation for as long as either of us would have liked, and, clutching his book and promising to get in touch with me, he left the room. It was some months before he telephoned me, ostensibly to tell me how much he had enjoyed the book, though I could sense that he wanted to talk about the past, in the way that so many old folk do. Hence, a few days later, I made my way to his little bachelor flat on the edge of Norwich, to be greeted with the warmest of handshakes and a beaming 95-year-old smile.

Uncle Jim must surely have been one of the first people to have been born in the twentieth century, for he made his entry into the world at just ten or fifteen minutes after midnight on January 1st, 1901. He was the youngest of four sons and a daughter born to the Burgoyne family, who farmed a little way outside Docking in the direction of Burnham Market.

I immediately knew that I was in the presence of a very modest man, quiet and self-effacing almost to the point of shyness. He could not understand why I should be interested in his early life. "It was so ordinary," he said. I assured him that it was that very fact that made it interesting, for people of today can know little of the lives of our antecedents of a century ago.

It soon became clear that he had inherited his shyness from his mother, who had to summon up her courage every week to attend the Mothers' Meeting in the village. It was held in the cottage home of one of the members, and her presence was an integral part of the proceedings, for she habitually read to the other women from one of the family's collection of "good" books. Every week, self-consciousness had to give way to the call of duty. Then, if she was unwell or had other engagements, one of the boys would be sent to deputise for her. Jim never forgot the first time he was called upon to carry out this duty.

Carrying Louisa M Alcott's *Little Women* in a satchel, he rode miserably across the fields to the village and tied up his pony at the blacksmith's. Then came the apprehensive pause before the cottage door as the strange up-and-down intonation of the country women's voices came to him from behind the potted geraniums on the window-sill. He felt sick, but there was no escape. He lifted the latch and stepped into the musty, fusty, cosy cottage smell – the sort of smell that goes with the ticking of a grandfather clock, just as apple sauce goes with pork. There was a sudden hush, he felt his face burning, and then came the dreaded welcome, the endearments, the surprise at his growth and his likeness to his mother. It was a relief when the reading began, and it says much for the quality of Louisa's writing that his love for *Little Women* arose out of, and survived, the terrors of that day.

Just as their inherent shyness was a legacy from their mother, so Jim and his brothers inherited from their father a strong lack of enthusiasm for organised team sports. He, it seems, had attended a public school where participation in such games was *de rigueur,* and perhaps it was the compulsory nature of those activities which raised in him a feeling of resentment. In any case, he did not take kindly to having a hard, speedily-dispatched ball bouncing around his head or striking him on the shins, nor did he appreciate being buried under a struggling mass of boyhood in a rugby scrum.

For the boys there were many country pursuits to take the place of ball games, and it goes without saying that riding came naturally to them. They learnt to ride by breaking in (and falling off) a wild and wilful Welsh pony named Timmy. They acquired many a bump in the process, but it was no good looking for sympathy for, in their world, falling off was regarded as the fault of the rider and certainly not of the pony.

In those early days they did not regard riding as an amusement in the way that children do today, but merely as a means of getting about. They used Timmy, in fact, as many other children would use a bicycle. They rode to fetch fish from the man who got them straight from the boats; they rode across the park to tell the blacksmith that a horse needed shoeing; and they rode into Docking to take boots and shoes to Mr Skerry for repair.

Freddy Skerry was a great attraction because of his size – or, I should say, lack of it. Indeed, so diminutive was he that he became known as "The Docking Dwarf". It was he, also, who was reputed to have discovered a way to make a hundred pairs of shoes in a day, and who, for a suitable monetary consideration, was prepared to divulge his secret. History does not record whether anybody took up the offer, but the answer was quite simple – merely take a hundred pairs of boots and cut off all the tops.

Apart from the boys' routine rides, there was to be one occasion when Timmy was to fulfil a most unexpected, but extremely welcome, purpose. It was on the day that Edward and Richard came to tea. Edward and Richard were the Vicar's grandsons and were spending part of their summer holiday at the Vicarage. Jim's father, in spite of his dislike of ball games, calmly announced that he had invited them to the farm "to play a game of cricket". Jim

FREDDY SKERRY.—THE DOCKING DWARF

and his brothers were appalled. They couldn't play cricket – they could neither bat, nor bowl, nor catch a ball, and they didn't even know the rules. The visitors were probably experts.

The boys' worst fears were realised. A single wicket was set up on the lawn and the "home side" were invited to bat first. Edward and Richard did not spare them. Their wickets were shattered almost before their bats were lifted. Then, when it was the visitors' turn to bat, it soon became apparent that even the distant greenhouses were under threat. It was, Jim told me, "our first encounter with the harshness of the outside world".

Eventually, relief came in the form of the tea interval, with Mother bringing out the sandwiches and sponge cakes for the two teams to picnic on the grass. The visitors ate heartily, but the home side showed little appetite, for there was more cricket to come after the interval. Fortunately, however, things suddenly took a turn for the better when Edward and Richard asked if they might have a ride on Timmy. Thankful for the respite from that beastly cricket ball, the brothers readily agreed and saddled the pony. What followed was sheer bliss. They had no thought that Timmy would avenge them, but avenge them he did. He threw them both, after a short but, to their hosts, delectable exhibition of saddle-holding and mane-clinging. They were both invited to remount, but they declined. So Jim and his brothers, in turn, did so, and galloped about to show their mastery.

"It wasn't such a bad afternoon after all," said Jim.

Though having no great liking for sports and team games, especially those which involved any form of flying ball, the boys were not physically soft – their daily preoccupations saw to that. Once they had outgrown the imaginative pastimes of infancy, their main employments were gardening and, not surprisingly, farming, and they took to them partly from inclination but, even more, for reasons of economic necessity. Jim's pocket money was threepence a week; it had been that right from the outset, and the passage of the years had brought him not even the smallest increase. Even in those earlier days, thirteen shillings a year could hardly be regarded as a princely sum, and the fact that each year brought seven family birthdays meant that a tight rein on their spending was called for during the rest of the year. It is true that a slight relief had come one year when, having bought for their father a pair of enormous spill-holders of brown glazed earthenware, with ears of corn entwined about their necks, they were told by their parents that they would much prefer home-made gifts rather than expensive purchases from the shops. Hence, pen-wipers, needle books and other things which they could stitch or glue together became their regular offerings to Mother and Father. For sister and brothers, however, etiquette decreed that a shop-bought article was required, and that, of course, needed money. Hence, the decision was made to "turn professional" and become market gardeners.

Almost since birth each one of them had possessed his own flower garden, at times cultivated with ferocious energy and at others totally neglected. For their new project, however, a greater area of land was required, so an approach was made to Father. He, no doubt thinking it to be good training for the future, heartily approved of the idea, but laid down certain conditions. Everything must be done in a business-like manner, with full and detailed accounts being kept – and they must pay the market rent. So the four boys went into business, and Michaelmas Day found them duly gathered together outside their father's study, ready to settle their landlord's dues and demands for their eighth of an acre.

Though this new venture was destined to achieve a modicum of success, it began with a devastating experience which, in its turn, was to teach the boys a salutary lesson which Jim, for one, never forgot. The boundaries of their holding were marked out with stones, and it was not long before they noticed that a large pear tree, which habitually carried a good crop of fruit, grew not more than a foot outside their boundary line. They thought of the many customers to whom they could sell the fruits of that tree if only it was on their land. The temptation was too great. They set to work and moved the stones so that the tree could be theirs. They felt no shame over this act of dishonesty, for they felt sure that nobody on Earth would notice. As they expected, nobody on Earth seemed to notice or to care. But God noticed and was not pleased.

It was Ash Wednesday, and they were taken to Church for the Commination Service, which was a feature of religious life in those days. Jim had to explain, for I knew nothing of such things.

"It was sheer Hellfire and brimstone," he told me. "A tirade of threats of divine vengeance against all sinners".

It was the first time the boys had attended a Commination Service, and they were quite unprepared for what was to come. There was the preacher, sombre of face, facing his congregation. Then he spoke:

"Cursed is he that removeth his neighbour's landmark. Amen".

The words struck into the bodies of the four brothers as though they were rods of steel. The boys were panic-stricken. It was as much as they could do to wait for the service to end, and then they ran as fast as their legs could carry them back to their holding, where they hastily restored the stone boundary to its original position.

It was clear to me that, even after the passage of so many years, Jim still felt the shame of their action that day, for it was written across his face. I could do no more than reassure him that very few of us complete our lifespan without collecting, on the way, the odd skeleton in the cupboard.

In the event, they need never have engaged in their sinful subterfuge for, when the tree bore its next crop of pears, their father gave them permission to put to their own use any which overhung their land. These found a ready market in the shape of the painters who seemed to be eternally crawling over the long line of greenhouses. Those men were also ready customers for bantams' eggs at ninepence a dozen and cockerels at one and sixpence. At this point in his narrative, Jim proceeded to describe in great detail how, with their own hands, the boys used to kill the cockerels "in the right professional manner". I wished he had spared me the gory details, and I have no desire to transfer them into print. Farming, I fear, can be a heartless business for all concerned.

The boys also did well with a pig which they bought for ten shillings and, after spending another ten shillings for food to fatten it, sold it for thirty shillings – a handy profit! Even this success, however, was as nothing compared with that achieved with two turkeys they managed to rear, out of a clutch of five eggs sat upon by a bantam hen. Three of them mysteriously died, but the two survivors, one a 17-pounder, were sold to the family's solicitor.

The years went by and, gradually and almost imperceptibly, the four boys became men. The eldest, indeed, had taken unto himself a wife, which meant that there were eight adults dependent upon the farm for a livelihood. All four boys wanted to stay in farming, for it was the only life they had known, but the industry was in a very depressed state, and there was no way in which they could acquire more land. It seemed a forlorn situation until suddenly, in 1925, Fate intervened and provided a solution, albeit in a most heartbreaking manner.

The boys had an uncle who was farming in another part of the county, and it was his sudden death, in the most tragic of circumstances, that brought about a change in the family's prospects. He left a widow and a 3-year-old child, but the farm needed stronger hands than theirs, so it was decided that Jim and his married brother and sister-in-law should take over the running of the place. Thus it was that they moved to their late uncle's farm – not far outside North Walsham, on the road to Bacton. The little fatherless child was, of course, Naomi, with whom, five years later, I was to have my brief encounter. It will be seen that Jim was, strictly speaking, her cousin rather than the Uncle of whom she became so fond. It was the great difference in their ages – for he was then 24 – and the fact that he was also her Godfather that led her to regard him as her Uncle Jim.

During the many hours that I sat with Jim and listened to his reminiscences, one thought was uppermost in my mind – I wanted news of Naomi. But each time I tried to talk of her, he deftly steered me away to some other topic, and I could not deny him, for he was so happy reliving his past. It was at this point in his narrative, however, that I was able to ask the question that I had been wanting to put to him for so long: How had she got on with the malady which had made her "unwell"?

"Oh, fine," he said. "A few weeks and she was as right as rain".

"And where is she now?" I asked.

His face immediately told me that it was a question better left unasked. I would have given anything at that moment to have been able to take back those words. But, after a very slight pause, he gave me my answer.

She had always wanted to go into nursing, he told me, but when the Second World War broke out she was still only 17, and neither he nor her mother relished the thought of her leaving home. Early the following year, 1940, knowing that her heart was set upon it, they finally agreed, and she set off for London to become a nurse in a hospital in the East End (only a short distance, incidentally, from where, at the same time, I was engaged in my medical studies). They soon knew, from her letters, that she was doing what she wanted to do and, in spite of the air raids, she was enjoying every minute. But then, on September 12th, 1940, she had gone with other nurses to have tea at an A.B.C. teashop when the sirens suddenly wailed their warning. It was just a single bomb that was dropped, but it scored a direct hit on the teashop, reducing it to nothing more than a heap of rubble. There were no survivors.

At that point we both sat silently for what seemed an eternity. Then, Jim decided we needed a cup of tea and disappeared into his kitchenette to put the kettle on.

One of my later visits was just a few days before his 96th birthday and, though mentally alert, he had long lost the vigour of youth. No longer able to wield a pen, he had dictated a few thoughts to one of his carers, who had then tapped them out on her word processor. Frail he may have been, but he was a man at peace with the world. These were his words:

> *I have never felt any wish to go back to farming, but I still have an affection for growing crops, and it is their submissive part in the business rather than that of the labouring farmer which appeals to me. I love nothing more than to lean upon a gate and watch things grow, but I have no wish to sit upon a tractor. I will always be at home in a farmyard, where I can admire the young stock with the dew fresh upon their noses, yet I have no feeling of envy towards their master. After all, my main purpose in life was to make a living. Now, having sufficient for my needs, I am content to let others take their turn. But towards the soil, and the working of it, I can never be a stranger.*

January 2nd.

Wymondham Market Cross.

The sum subscribed towards the restoration fund of Wymondham Market Cross amounts, according to the latest announcement, to £104 15s 6d, which, however, is stated to be insufficient, and hence the appeal to the public for more help is continued by the promoters of the movement.

We somewhat wish that we could give the entreaty a heartier recommendation than we are honestly able to do, believing that a fine open square would be of infinitely greater importance to the town than the plastering up of an old building, from which modern alterations take away the associations of antiquity, and which seems literally, as well as figuratively, to stand in the road to advantages to which it must necessarily continue a top-heavy obstruction.

Norfolk News, January 2nd, 1864

The Road to the Station.

January 17th, 1888 saw the completion of Norwich's Foundry Bridge, fifty feet in width and built at a cost of £12,032. It was the final piece in the jigsaw of changes which had been taking place in that area of the City throughout the preceding 45 years. It was, furthermore, the second bridge to bear that name, replacing one which had been erected in 1844, and it marked the completion of surely one of the greatest transformations ever known in the City's long history.

It had all begun in 1843 with the coming of the railway, and there had been quite a battle to keep that new-fangled means of transport outside the perimeter of the City. The developers wanted to bring their track across the river and build their station at some central point. Tombland had always been the historic centre, but the idea of siting it there was quickly rejected. Then there was the fanciful dream of driving their lines into the Close, but that was a non-starter from the outset.

In order to appreciate the difficulties involved, it is necessary to visualise that particular part of Norwich as it was a century and a half ago, and, accustomed as we are to its present built-up state, picturing the scene in the 1840s is not a simple matter. To begin with, there was no Thorpe Road or Prince of Wales Road; there was no Riverside Road. There was, in fact, almost nothing which could be described as man-made – with the possible exception of the iron foundry which was to give its name to the new bridge. The River Wensum was, of course, the City's eastern line of defence and, all the way from the Boom Towers, where King Street ran along the river bank, northwards to Bishop Bridge, there had never been a road entering Norwich.

All the land adjoining the river between the Cathedral Close and King Street had been the property of the Greyfriars, and with the Dissolution of the Monasteries it had been divided up into market gardens, orchards and hop fields. There had been, for some time, a short cut from the Yarmouth road, leading to a wooden bridge across the Wensum and then to a narrow lane known to

Bishop Bridge, the city's original outlet to the Yarmouth road, which began its journey over the slopes of Mousehold.

local residents simply as "the path through the hop gardens".

The land on the eastern side of the river, outside the City boundary, was wild and undeveloped, and that was as far as the railway was allowed to come. The people of old Norwich were shy of the snorting monster that had been created – they were, indeed, alarmed by it. What is more, they had no need of it, for the goods the City produced could well be sent on their way along the waters of the Wensum or by means of "the heavy wagon to Birmingham", which used to run from its collection point on Tombland, just outside the Ethelbert Gate.

It was the "Yarmouth & Norwich Railway Company" which brought the first smoke-belching engines and their clattering trucks to the fringe of the City, and it started in rather modest fashion. By the time the first cuttings had been dug and the bridges built, the railway amounted to a twenty-mile stretch from the old Vauxhall Pleasure Gardens, just outside Yarmouth, to the spot in what was then the County parish of Thorpe where the Yarmouth road, leaving Norwich by Bishop Bridge, started its climb over the slopes of Mousehold. It was the area which, in earlier times, had seen some of the fiercest fighting in Kett's Rebellion, and it was there, on a flat area of land, that they built their "station". This edifice, in itself, was an innovation, for the local folk were accustomed to horse-drawn transport, which they always associated with stables. It is said that it was the Company's knowledge of this fact that caused them to build their station in a style which, as far as possible, resembled stabling. It was basically a single-storey structure, built of weather-boarding and topped with a clock tower and dovecote. It stood much nearer to the river's edge than does the Thorpe Station of today, with its frontage facing towards Pull's Ferry.

By the end of October in 1843, their track was able to carry "an engine with ballast trucks running from the Yarmouth end to assist the excavation". And the people of Norwich turned out in force to inspect this fantastic new creation.

The local newspaper, in the wonderfully descriptive style in which reporters so lovingly wrote in those days, summed it all up: "Its marvellous facility in whirling along any number of loaded wagons elicited exclamations of astonishment from many hundreds of Norwich people who went out to see it".

Eventually, on April 12th, 1844, the Directors of the Railway ran a ceremonial passenger train from Norwich to Yarmouth, accompanied not only by Major-General Pasley, the Government Inspector, but also by none other than the Lord Bishop of Norwich. The age of the train had arrived – but it was to be another twenty years before it was to come any nearer to the heart of Norwich.

They must have been years of acute inconvenience, for the new railway station was opposite the least accessible part of Norwich. It was readily apparent that some sort of approach road to and from the centre of the City was required, but the big problem was which route it should take. Eventually it was decided that, by utilising part of "the path through the hop gardens" and then an old alley, known as Rose Lane, which ran from King Street towards the river, a new thoroughfare from the wooden bridge could be provided, running in a sweeping curve to the point where King Street met up with Tombland. Thus was born the road which they named after the Prince of Wales.

For most of my life I have had a great affection for Prince of Wales Road, although I now feel pity for the sad old thoroughfare which, under pressure from modern traffic, seems not to know where it is heading. Some of my love, I admit, may have stemmed

The original Foundry Bridge, built in 1844, and, in the background, the first Thorpe Station, designed to resemble stabling and set at an angle to face towards Pull's Ferry.

Prince of Wales Road, built in 1862, with the unfinished Prince of Wales Terrace in the distance. The building on the right was Mills and Underwood's Malt Vinegar Factory.

The austere modern face of Prince of Wales Road.

from the fact that it was the first part of the City I encountered when I was taken there on my early boyhood visits from North Walsham. The fact that it was something special, however, is borne out by R.H. Mottram who, writing in 1952, described it as "the one street in Norwich that can take four lines of traffic, even modern buses, and does so".

Though it was the youngest of the Norwich thoroughfares, there were parts where it carried an occasional glint of the past. On the corner by Rose Lane a large showroom full of modern motor cars took over the premises where builders of horse-drawn carriages had earlier plied their trade, and dotted along the road there was a clutch of garages taking the place in society formerly filled by coachbuilders, cab proprietors and the like.

There were certain astute citizens who foresaw the likelihood of the development of the area and who, in the preceding years, had bought up such pieces of land as they could acquire. They were the ones to benefit financially when the time came and they could start erecting properties for speculative sale. Some, it is said, were "thrown up" – perhaps that was the case with numbers 47 to 51 on the south side which, as late as 1923, collapsed for no apparent reason.

Surely the same could not be said of those on the northern side, particularly those impressive buildings in that graceful sweep at the top of the road. Prince of Wales Terrace they called it, and they were the properties of professional men, doctors and lawyers, who found it convenient to "live above the shop". Three storeys they had, with attics at the top and basements with areas and pavement-level gratings – surely destined to make many a maidservant old before her time!

But there is no doubt about it – Norwich was proud of Prince of Wales Road. Soon it became the favourite promenade, after work on weekdays and again on Sundays, for folk who had never before had such luxury as the new road offered. All the way they would go, from Foundry Bridge up to the new Bank and the Agricultural Hall; through to London Street, which had at last shed its Cockey Lane past and taken upon itself a new image of respectability; and then onward into the Market Place. For the poorer members of society, long cooped up in their crowded hovels, it was like a first glimpse of Heaven.

The eyes of the more well-to-do, however, were directed further afield, over Foundry Bridge and into the immediate countryside

St. Lawrence Court, off St. Benedict's Street, typical of the confined living areas from which the occupants were glad to escape to promenade along the new road.

Yards and tiles of old St. Giles', where the residents received very little sunlight. Photograph taken from the tower of St. Giles' Church.

which lay on the other side of the Wensum. The fledgling Yarmouth & Norwich Railway had become the Great Eastern, with its grand new station, built in 1886 opposite the new bridge, and full of Victorian solidity and splendour. The original outlet from Norwich, over Bishop Bridge and Mousehold, and onwards to the coast, became the "old" Yarmouth road. Convenience decreed, however, that Prince of Wales Road and Foundry Bridge, though built purely to serve the needs of the railway, should become the new gateway to that part of the county. The new Thorpe Road, in essence a short cut to Yarmouth, blossomed out with substantial villa residences behind iron palings and flint walls. Up the hill and ever outwards the new properties sprang up, past Clarence Road and the Rosary, Cremorne Gardens and the Redan Inn, spawning new roads bearing celebrated names of the age – names like Stanley, Wellesley and Cotman.

Before long, even greater changes were to come. It can be said that Prince of Wales Road was the result of forward planning by the City Fathers, but other unforeseen consequences were to call for dramatic remedies. First of all, the movement of the population so far outside the old City meant that they were now living far from their workplaces, and some form of transport was needed. It was then that the trams made their controversial entry upon the scene and began something like thirty-five uneasy years up and down the city streets. Happily accepted by those who were to use them in their daily travels, they were an unwelcome intrusion to others. The traders of Prince of Wales Road resented the loss of their previously unquestioned right to park their delivery vehicles outside their premises; others, long accustomed to the peace of horse-drawn traffic, found the cacophony of the iron monsters an insufferable assault upon their quality of life. The professional men in those splendid villas at the top of the road moved out, the lawyers into the quieter confines of such places as the Close, and the doctors further afield to the new districts in which their patients had gone to live.

Then, yet another problem was to arise, particularly for those who had built their splendid new homes in those eastern areas on either side of the new Thorpe Road. And it was the Railway, which had brought such sudden prosperity into their lives, that now threatened to destroy the futures they had planned for themselves. It was, in fact, the very success of the Railway that caused the problem, for with success there came the need for more trains and

The second Thorpe Station, built 1886. Photograph taken in 1914.

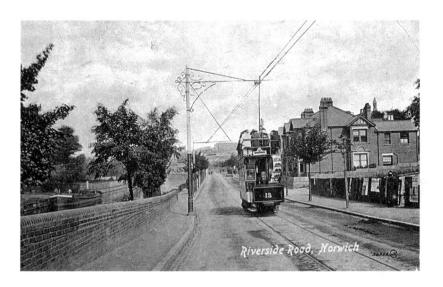

Riverside Road, photographed in 1921.

track, more engineering sheds and marshalling yards. With all this extra activity there inevitably came more smoke, and it was that by-product which set alarm bells ringing in the minds of the local doctors. "Too much pollution," they said. "The health of people living nearby will suffer – they would be well-advised to move to other parts of the city".

The mere fact of moving would probably not have been too much of a problem, but how could they sell their existing homes while such a health hazard hung over them? In today's world, such a situation would quite probably bring forth much talk of "negative equity" and a collapse of the housing market. There has long been a saying, however, that "when one door closes, another opens", and that is exactly what happened on this occasion.

At that time, of course, there was no County Hall, and local government affairs were dealt with in parish halls or, at the top of the tree, at the Shirehall. Such a situation, however, had become steadily more unworkable, and a great need was felt for a site where all the various County Council departments could operate in better conditions and in close contact with each other. What better solution could have been found than those lovingly-built, sturdy Victorian houses around Clarence Road and Stracey Road? The door had opened most fortuitously and, before long, Education and Health, Architects and Surveyors, Police and Transport all found homes where the previous tenants had expected to live out their retirement.

And what of them? They took themselves off to places where the air was fresher, and where the view from their windows was greener. Many, indeed, went further along the Yarmouth Road to the splendidly independent village of Thorpe St. Andrew which, with its peaceful Green by the river, earned for itself the soubriquet of "The Richmond of Norfolk", and where their only contact with the Railway was the modest, but convenient, Whitlingham Station.

Peter Eade – Budding Doctor.

Peter Eade was born on January 19th, 1825, in the parish of Acle, where his father was in practice as a doctor. He was the only son in a family of five children and was the third successive generation of Peter Eades, for both his father and his grandfather (formerly rector of Stow Bedon) had carried the same Christian name. He was to know little of the place of his birth, however, for it was only a few months later that the family moved to the prosperous and well-populated village of Blofield. There, in that parish of some twelve hundred souls, his father practised his profession for some 35 years before retiring to Norwich, where he died in 1867. It was an admirable situation for a doctor of those times, for there were many prosperous and well-to-do residents who eagerly welcomed the arrival in their midst of a man of such culture and learning and who soon held both the man and his splendid family in high regard. And it was there that the young Peter Eade was to spend the early years of his life – a life which, unbeknown to anybody at that time, was to have such a salutary and long lasting effect on the development of the city of Norwich.

The world in which Peter Eade grew up was a very different one from that which we know today. Amongst minor things, those were the days of rush candles for kitchen and night use, with tinder boxes and brimstone matches; of tallow candles with cotton wicks and their accompanying snuffers and snuffer trays; and of wax candles being jealously guarded for special occasions.

In charge of law and order they had their own parish constable until the establishment in Norfolk of the Rural (County) Police under Sir Robert Peel's Act in 1839. To mete out punishment for minor misdemeanours, Blofield had its own stocks, in a central and most public situation, and Peter Eade well remembered seeing them occupied (for drunkenness, he believed) by an otherwise respected pillar of society. "And a very odd and striking sight it was," he recalled, "to see this strong and powerfully built man sitting on the ground with his ankles locked in the stocks, and exposed to the pitying gaze of every passer-by".

Blofield was an "open" parish. In other words, the land was not in the ownership of one large landowner, but rather spread about amongst a fair number of small farmers and a score or so of market gardeners, who became what have been described as the "happy possessors of three acres and a cow".

In "close" parishes, where most of the men were in the employ of one major landowner, great efforts were made to prevent such men from building cottages within the parish boundary, for parishes were at that time separately rated, and the occupying labourers would thus become chargeable to the rates. Instead, pressure was brought to bear on them to find a place of residence in another parish, to which they would then belong. This, of course, relieved the landowner's parish of much expense, but it often caused much daily hardship to the labourers, who then found it necessary to travel long distances to and from their place of employment.

No such restriction could be enforced in an "open" parish, however, and thus most of the freeholders of Blofield erected a small house or cottage, where they became extremely independent in both their way of life and their speech. Many of them, sadly, developed the habit of raising money by mortgaging their little properties for all they could get, which often resulted in their living in rather more straitened circumstances than their landless brethren. Nevertheless, they were always looked up to by these latter as "proprietors" – and they were certainly more thoughtful and intelligent, no doubt because of their constant mental efforts to retain their independence.

Farming in those days was a very prosperous occupation for the freeholders, with rents being high and vacant farms often eagerly competed for. For the labourers, however, wages were low, and it was the accepted practice for them to gather in groups at the conclusion of harvest and visit the more well-to-do members of the parish to beg for "largesse". Peter Eade's father was always high on the list of people to be visited for this purpose, not only because of the high esteem which his profession brought with it, but also because he was a freeholder with several acres of land. Throughout his life, the young Peter retained memories of parties of men, some from Blofield and others from nearby parishes, assembling upon the lawn in front of his father's house and, after receiving a harvest gift, forming up in a circle and lustily "hollering largesse". This practice later gave way to the more recently remembered custom of the farmer giving his men and their families a harvest supper, either in his own house or in one of his barns. Then there was the annual Michaelmas Fair which, though modest by today's standards, attracted most of the parishioners of Blofield, together with many from such nearby parishes as Bradeston, Brundall and Strumpshaw.

The Eade family's acres were always intensively cultivated, though not with the conventional crops favoured by the other freeholders. The days of mass-produced drugs and medicines were still far in the future, and the doctor of that time had perforce to make up his own draughts and mixtures, his pills and powders, and his liniments and ointments. Most doctors obtained the various ingredients from wholesale druggists, but Dr. Eade was an exception in that, as far as possible, he grew his own. Fortunately, he drew the line at hemlock, but such things as poppies, henbane and roses were regular crops in his fields. The white poppies, in fact, regularly covered an acre or more, for it was from them that, with careful preparation, came the *Extractum Papaveris* – the wonder drug of the age! The stems and leaves were carefully gathered, then mashed in a large iron mortar, from which the juice was evaporated over a fire until it reached the consistency of a soft fluid – just firm enough to make pills. The young Peter Eade recalled many tedious hours spent in this wearisome activity.

All the while, standing like a sentinel above the surrounding countryside, there was the splendid Parish Church of St Andrew, with its tangible reminders of centuries of history. Some of the later members of the Paston family were buried there – Edward Paston (who was attached to the Court of Henry the Eighth), his wife and their nine children, their memory enshrined in a wall monument. High in the tower was the peal of six bells, one of which was reputed to have been cast when Shakespeare was still a boy. Many years later, in 1916, the church was destined to be further embellished with a window dedicated to the doctor's son who grew up in the parish – but much was to happen before that day.

The living of Blofield was in the gift of Caius College, Cambridge, and was of considerable value; hence it was always given to one of the Fellows of the College. This practically ensured that the Rector, though handicapped by inexperience and bachelorhood, was at least a man of high class as regards education, position and mental calibre. It has to be said, furthermore, that the question of class was mirrored right through the congregation.

To begin with, there were 400 sittings in the church but, though this was frequently less than the number needed, there was no question of a worshipper taking a pew which appeared to be unoccupied. Each member of the parish had a designated position in society, and this was reflected in the position in which he was permitted to sit in the church.

The north and south aisles were fitted with tall pews for the families of the "better classes", and the reputed quality of these "owners" began at the top of the aisle and gradually diminished downwards to its lowest part, where many of the gentlemen's servants were located. The nave was fitted with rows of open benches, those on the right of the central aisle being allocated to the poor women of the parish and those on the left to the poor men – it was only amongst the poorer classes that the sexes were segregated.

Below the reading-desk there was a sturdy pew for the parish clerk, who very audibly read the responses, gave out the hymns, and loudly said the "Amens". The choir was voluntary and was seated at the lower end of the church. As there was no organ or harmonium, the initial note to the hymns was usually given out by a clarinet.

Although most of the parishioners, however lowly their station, accepted the class-ridden system of seating in the church, there were, nevertheless, occasions when disputed claims of tenure gave rise to bickering and, at times, heated arguments. One such dispute, concerning one of the more highly-rated pews, lived long in the memories of the congregation, for it was settled without a single word being spoken. A newcomer to the parish, a man of diminutive build and peaceful nature, decided to stake his claim by arriving at church long before the service and claiming his right simply by means of occupancy. It so happened that the rightful "owner" of the pew did not attend church that day, nor, indeed, on the two following Sundays. By this time, the newcomer was beginning to feel that his ploy had been successful. On the fourth Sunday, however, all this was to change. He had, as usual, gone early to occupy what he now regarded as "his" pew, but, a mere couple of minutes before the service was due to start, the rightful owner put in an appearance. Neither man spoke, but the latecomer, being a very tall and muscular man, simply leaned over the side of the tall pew, took hold of the intruder by the shoulders, and lifted him bodily out, depositing him on the floor of the aisle. He then entered the pew and seated himself "in his own", a proceeding not disputed by the ejected man.

It was against this background that the young Peter Eade set about the business of growing up. His was a somewhat sheltered existence for, until he reached the age of thirteen, he was educated at home with his four sisters under the tuition of a resident governess. In his latter years he questioned the wisdom of delaying his external schooling for so long, admitting that, as a single boy of twelve or thirteen, he had been "too masterful and troublesome" with his sisters and the governess. On the other hand, however, it was during that period of teaching at home that he had acquired the greater part of his knowledge of religious principles, for which he was to be grateful in later life.

It was in 1838 that he was sent to a highly-regarded educational establishment in Great Yarmouth known as the Proprietary Grammar School. Yarmouth was, at that time, a very different place from the one we know today. For one thing, it was much smaller, and the long row of buildings which now constitute Marine Parade was then only being built. There was neither a Wellington nor a Britannia Pier – merely a short jetty, opposite which stood the. old "Barking Smack" public house. There were no railway stations nor trams, transport being by horse coaches and a steamboat which took several hours to make the journey up the River Yare to Norwich. Most significantly of all, perhaps, there was no big fish market of the kind which was later destined to bring such prosperity to the town. Instead of being brought into the harbour, the fishing smacks at that time anchored near the beach and sent their cargoes of herring and mackerel ashore near the jetty in small boats. During the autumn fishing season, the sight which gave greatest delight to the thirteen-year-old boy was that of the boats being brought up to and on to the shore on the crests of the waves, and their bright silvery cargoes being given over to the waiting womenfolk, who took them away in baskets for removal in carts.

The Proprietary Grammar School was at Southtown on a site later occupied by the railway station, and Peter Eade remembered the building as being "large, well warmed by hot-water-pipes, and ventilated by numerous large raised windows". Even more vivid in his memory, however, was the misery of his first few days after arrival, and the intense homesickness that he experienced. As he confided to his diary:

> *This was not unnatural, launched as I was, for the first time in my life, amongst a hundred or more strange boys of varying sizes and ages, many bigger and older than myself, and most of them having previously undergone the same 'breaking-in' to which new boys seemed always to be subjected. This 'breaking-in' consisted of various petty personal injuries or provocations, and even of incitements to fight with other boys. Mainly owing to the petty tyranny constantly going on, I have always felt that my schooldays were the most unhappy of my whole life.*

The 'petty tyranny' suffered by young Peter could, indeed, have been even worse had it not been for the fact that, after a few months, two or three of the senior boys discovered that he possessed the talent to help them with the essays which they were periodically called upon to write. Henceforth, therefore, he would write the essays for them, and they, in return, would operate a mafia-like protection racket to guard him against the depredations of his hostile schoolmates.

But his greatest schoolday achievement was his mastery of Latin. This reached its pinnacle when, having progressed to one of the senior forms, he and his colleagues were given the holiday task of learning by heart the whole of Horace's Odes. I, myself, was a reasonable Latin scholar, but I am happy to admit that I was never confronted with Horace and his Odes, for I am reliably informed that they comprise nearly three thousand lines of varying length. Hence Peter Eade's great satisfaction at being one of just a few boys who accomplished that feat of memory and could repeat in class the whole, or any portion, of those Odes.

Regrettably, the same could not be said when it came to French, although this was through no fault of his own, for it was an age when a knowledge of modern languages was not considered to be of such importance to a well-educated man as it now is. After all, Britannia ruled the waves, most of the Map of the World was coloured pink and, if a foreigner wished to converse with an Englishman, it was up to him to learn our language. Hence their French master, though a most worthy and competent man, was fighting a losing battle in his efforts to teach them the intricacies of his native tongue.

Somehow Peter Eade managed to survive the rigours of school life until, in 1841, he reached his sixteenth birthday and his schooldays came to an end. With more than just a sigh of relief he returned to Blofield, where it had already been decided that he should follow his father into the medical profession. At that time it was still the custom that medical students should be apprenticed to some qualified medical practitioner and, accordingly, indentures binding him to his father as his pupil were duly executed. For the next three years, as he assisted his father, he learned much about general practice, particularly as regards pharmacy and the making-up of the various pills and potions.

He also learned something of minor surgery for, in the first year, his father had an older pupil, amongst whose responsibilities was the extraction of teeth. On one occasion this young gentleman, because of his faulty placement of the forceps, inadvertently removed two teeth simultaneously – the decayed tooth and the adjacent one. It should be remembered that this was before the days of anaesthetics, and the patient was wide awake throughout the proceedings. Hence, the mishap caused great consternation to both the operator and his assistant. As luck would have it, however, the surgery window was open at the time, and the sound tooth was hastily ejected through it. The unfortunate patient expressed his extreme surprise at the size of the gap left by a single tooth, but the guilty pair were able to keep their secret to themselves.

During the third year of his apprenticeship Peter Eade rode the seven miles to Norwich every day to attend the Norfolk and Norwich Hospital, where he had been entered by his father as a pupil and dresser under Mr John Greene Crosse, one of the most eminent surgeons at that time. This was to prove of great benefit in later years, although there were many times when he found his situation almost unbearable, for the amputation of limbs was very commonplace, and anaesthetics were still a dream of the future. It was on January 14th, 1847, in fact, that he recorded that the use of anaesthetics (known then as 'ethereal fumes') was introduced at the Norfolk and Norwich Hospital by a certain Dr. Hull for the extraction of teeth. It was not until December 30th of that year that chloroform was used for the first time in a surgical operation at that hospital.

Peter Eade, however, was never a man to give up, and in due course he completed his three-year apprenticeship to his father and prepared himself for the next stage in his training. To this end, he

Peter Eade as a young man.

proceeded to London, where he was entered as a medical student of King's College Hospital for the next three years. It was October, 1844, and his journey was made by coach and horses as far as Colchester and then on to London by the railway.

King's College had only a small number of rooms for resident students, and he was consequently placed in lodgings in a nearby street. This situation brought him a far greater amount of personal freedom and, with it, his first introduction to the social life of the medical world – and he found it very much to his liking. To begin with, there was the necessity of dining at some restaurant or other, many of which existed in the neighbourhood. A good dinner was obtainable for a shilling, with a penny extra for a glass of ale or porter, and a penny for the waiter. Frequently the students would dine at a well-known Fleet Street tavern, in a long, narrow, sanded-floored room, split up into little separate wooden compartments, each containing a small table. The budding doctor never forgot how they often dined off one of the specialities of the place, such as a pork chop and sausage, instead of the ordinary plate of meat. Then, for entertainment, there were the farces at the Adelphi. Peter Eade was enjoying his new life!

His enthusiasm for the social life of that time, however, always took second place to his work in the hospital, for he was a young man who invariably concentrated his mind on whatever objective he chose to pursue. He was a model student and, by the time he had achieved fully qualified medical status, he had acquired countless class prizes, scholarships, and gold and silver medals. (Yes, medical students really did win gold medals in those days!)

After all his successes at King's College, he had a great desire to continue his medical career in London, where he found life very congenial. Unfortunately for him, his financial means were decidedly limited, and then there was the fact that his father badly needed his assistance back in Norfolk. Hence, he returned to Blofield to consider and await events, and in the meantime to get some experience of general practice. It was to be a temporary measure, he said, for London had aroused his ambition, and he vowed to return there. The passage of time, however, can change all things, and so it proved for the young Doctor Eade. Fate decreed otherwise, a fact for which the City of Norwich should be eternally grateful.

(The story of Peter Eade's adult life begins on page 115)

February 8th.

Nobody's Road.

A Councillor complained at a County Council meeting that he had fallen in a pot-hole in a certain road, and he proposed that appropriate action should be taken to prevent a recurrence of such mishap. The Assistant County Surveyor, however, replied that it was not a "County" road and therefore they could not repair it.

February 8th, 1944.

There's a road runs back o' our village –
    Thas a mystery road that is;
That ain't repaired by nobody,
    An' nobody knows whose 'tis.
Now Betsy's eddicated, an' ses as how I'm wrong;
    If nobody they don't dew it, it must be done by some.

But I knows that that road isn't,
    An' tells her so, wot's more;
There's roads all round like that one,
    Why I knows three or four.
They used ter be repaired way back,
    When I worn't very old;
Surveyor had 'em mended up
    In days of frost and cold.

Then County Council took the roads,
    And R.D.C. were riled;
"What, give 'em all our roads?" they sed,
    O bor they did get wild!
So when they made the schedule,
    They went an' left some out;
An' thas caused all the trouble,
    An' all the roads without.
Nobody now to mend 'em, and nobody now to care.
    They calls it makin' progress, but that wholly make me swear!

Lucilla Reeve.

A Country Philosopher.

I wish I had known Charlie, but that would not have been possible, for he died before I was born. Even his surname is unknown to me, as is the village where he lived, but one thing I am certain about is that he was a man of Norfolk and a countryman to boot. And Victoria was his Queen.

I was told the story of Charlie many years ago by Arthur Whybrow, an elderly friend of many years standing, as I sat by his bed – the bed from which he was destined no more to rise. As he spoke, I made notes on a sheet of paper and, when I returned home, I tucked the paper in a cupboard with a mass of others which, I thought, might some day come in handy. The years went by and the sheet of paper lay completely forgotten in the cupboard until, quite by chance, I stumbled upon it while looking for something else. I sat down to read what I had written all those years ago.

At the top of the page was the date, February 21st, but with no mention of the year. That omission mattered little, however, for Arthur has been gone these many years. Hence I shall never know Charlie's surname, nor the village in which he lived, though I am sure it was one of those little places in the area around Worstead and North Walsham. Yes, I am sorry I never knew Charlie, but, thanks to Arthur, I feel almost as though I did.

Charlie was born in humble circumstances and never attained wealth or worldly position. By virtue of his natural character, however, and by sheer force of personality, he earned the love and respect of everybody throughout the community. His father had been a gamekeeper and one of the earliest Wesleyan Methodists in the village. Charlie became a thatcher, but that was only part of his life, for he became in many ways the general handyman of the district. He was hedger, ditcher, forester, roadman and "brusher", and, all the while, his work threw him into contact with animals, for which he had a great love.

He was tall, gnarled and grizzled, horny-handed by long years of laborious toil, bronzed by the sun and wind of nearly eighty summers and winters. Learned in the lore of the countryside, he had a keen understanding of birds and beasts, and a shrewd commonsense which was his most distinctive characteristic. He was, in short, that most splendid of all beings, a country philosopher, though he would never have called himself that and probably had no idea of the meaning of the word.

Except for a short period in his earlier years when he was a bellringer and attended the parish church, he was a lifelong Wesleyan and, for many years, chapel steward. While "taking the plate round" in the chapel, he thought nothing of holding up the proceedings to discuss the hymns and the sermon. In the general life of the community, he was always ready to help at village concerts, singing or reciting until he was well into his seventies. He was full to overflowing with native humour, which bubbled up into his everyday speech, and also deeply religious, a fact which caused the local vicar to enjoy a discussion and a little verbal sparring with him.

It was during one of their conversations that the clergyman remarked, "I am told that you sometimes preach, Charles".

"No, that I don't," replied Charlie. "I don't preach – but if the preacher don't turn up I sometimes say a few words".

"But," retorted the clergyman, "how can you explain the scriptures when it takes so much learning to understand them, and you have had but little education?"

"Well, thass like this here, Reverend." said Charlie. "On a fruit tree there's fruit all over – on the lower branches as well as on the top. Now, I can allus find enough to satisfy me on the lower branches, so I stop where I can git a firm foothold. I don't try and pluck fruit off the branches that I can't reach".

Charlie's pronouncements were liberally sprinkled with allegories and parables, mostly arising from his everyday surroundings and the things he witnessed in the countryside. There was an occasion when, because of a spell of bad weather, the superintendent minister had been somewhat neglectful as regards services in the chapel. At least, that was Charlie's opinion, and he remonstrated with the minister in no uncertain manner.

"If you've got a few sheep in the corner of a field with a hurdle or two round 'em." he said, "you don't neglect them and just tend the sheep in the yard".

He carried the analogy of the sheep even further in his strong support of work amongst the younger members of society. "If the shepherd tearke the lambs out o' the field," he said, "the sheep will always follow".

He had an abiding dislike of over-lengthy sermons. "Just long enough to get your message acrorst," he said. "There are some o' them preachers who do too much harrowin'. When you put the seed in, you only just want to cover it with soil. You don't want to keep harrowin' and harrowin' like some folk do, or you'll upset the seed you've sown".

Though a great believer in Temperance, he was not a teetotaller. "There may not be much goodness in alcohol," he said, "but I reckon a glass o' beer is like a bit o' grease on my old barrer – that mearke things go better". But he supported the preacher on Temperance Sunday, complimenting him with, "You've done your duty in warning the people. If the watchman sees the enemy coming and gives the warning, he clears his own soul".

"Thass a load o' old squit," said a sceptic villager nearby. "We han't got no soul – we're just like hosses".

Charlie was indignant. "Now, just you listen to me," he said. "If you put a hoss in a neighbour's field of cabbages, when you want to get him out you'll have the devil and all trouble. But if *you* were to go into your neighbour's field of cabbages and heard the gate click, you'd be out like a shot. You've got a conscience – thass the difference between you and a hoss".

At Election time, Charlie's voting intentions were always a secret between him and the ballot box. On one occasion, the local landowner was standing, and much pressure was put upon him to cast his vote in favour of the Master. "We've all got to vote for him," they said. "Can we count on you?"

"I never tell no-one who I vote for," replied Charlie, "not even my missus".

Then, as if to settle the matter, he added: "Anyway, whoever heard of a tug-of-war where they wanted everyone to get hold of the same end of the rope?"

Yes, I have a feeling I would have liked Charlie.

March.

The Fust Butterfly.

There he go, a-flutterin' by,
The year's fust little butterfly,
A tortoiseshell, there in the sun;
I s'pus he think the winter's done.
Tha's arly yit, though warm an bright -
I reckon that might freeze t'night.
But that don't worry him, that fare -
Jus' see him now, a-settin' there . . .
. . . Them colours on his wings, they shine
Like jew'les, they dew; they look so fine
Wi' bands o' red an' bands o' white
An' black an' yaller, an' so bright
Along the edge them blue spots showin'
Like eyes on peacock's feathers glowin' . . .
Ah, he's a beauty! Orf he go
A-dancin' down the garden now
T'find another sunny spot
T'spreed his wings, as like as not.
A maaster-piece t'me that fare -
All winter t'rew he jus' hung there
In my ole shud, wi' wings shut tight,
An now he's come t'life oright!
Ah, evra year when March come round
There's new life comin' from the ground,
A-waakenin' like that butterfly . . .
Tha's good t'see him flutterin' by.

John Kett

The small tortoiseshell, usually the first butterfly to visit our gardens.

The brimstone, often a challenger as it emerges from hibernation.

March 7th.

Only a Game.

The first week in March was traditionally the time for the Paston School's Annual Cross-country Run. It was not an event which I anticipated with any great degree of enthusiasm, and its only redeeming factor was that it took place just once a year. I must stress that my apathy towards that amble through the countryside to Felmingham and back did not stem from any dislike of sport in general, for the reverse was the case. Wednesday and Saturday afternoons were the highlights of my week, for it was then that we engaged in football and cricket, both of which were much to my liking. Even athletics came within my compass, but I was a sprinter. Anything up to 220 yards was pleasurable, but the four-mile trek on Cross-country Day (5½ miles for the seniors) was a bit of a bore.

I remember little of the four Cross-country Runs in which I took part, except a little incident towards the end of my first appearance. I was coming back under the railway bridge and towards the School when there came a full-throated roar of encouragement from a group of men standing outside Starling's Garage. They were presumably acquaintances of my father, for they gave out with loud shouts of "Well done, young Baggie", "Keep it up, young Baggie", and then, "Come on; now give us a sprint to the finish".

The warmth of their encouragement sent into my mind the thought that I was about to be the winner. It was a totally stupid thought for, though I could see nobody ahead of me in the run in through the School gates, we had been sent off at 10-second intervals, and I couldn't remember having overtaken anybody on the way. Nevertheless, I gave them the sprint for which they had asked, arriving at the finishing line as though I had just completed a hundred yards. I was not quite the winner; I finished, in fact, in 52nd place. I suppose that fact, set coldly down in print, does not appear very impressive, but I consoled myself with the thought that, as there had been 105 starters, I had at least finished in the top half!

At least I had taken part willingly. Even if participation had been optional I would still have been there, for to 'chicken out' would have been to cause a certain loss of face amongst one's peers. Yet, even at that early age, my heart went out to those boys who had no inclination towards sport and to whom such activities brought both physical and mental torture. It was the same with football and cricket, for the School was divided into four Houses, each of which put out four teams for each sport.

The Fourth Eleven was inevitably a motley collection of youngsters. Some were new arrivals whose capabilities had not yet been assessed; others were those who lacked talent but were happy to do the best they could – and then there were those who would have been much happier going home and doing their prep.

It was against one such team that I suffered the most humiliating experience of my cricketing career, the details of which have, until now, been a closely guarded secret. I was fifteen at the time and already playing in the First Eleven for both Nelson House and the School but, on the day in question, a scheduled School match had been cancelled, for reasons which now escape me. Junior House matches between Nelson and Hoste were to go ahead, however, so I strolled up to the School Field to run my eye over them. There, in the corner near the road, the Fourth Elevens were preparing for battle under the watchful eye of our House Master, the much-loved 'Cherry' Harris. Seeing me, he immediately beckoned me towards him.

"Just the man I want," he said. "We're one short. Greenacre has gone home with a bilious attack". (How strange that he should always have his bilious attacks on sport afternoons!)

I had mixed feelings about the situation but, within minutes, there I was, opening the batting for Nelson. I watched the diminutive bowler amble up to the wicket, put his arm over and release the ball into free flight. The trouble was that it went extremely high in the air, and I lost track of it amongst the background of black clouds which hung over the Ground. Eventually it came down and bounced barely half-way along the pitch, and it was then that I first became aware that we were not playing with a proper cricket ball, but with one of those sorbo rubber ones which possessed rather exaggerated bouncing properties. Up it went again in its skyward trajectory, though this time not so far as to prevent me from keeping my eye on it. I prepared myself for its second descent, fully prepared to sweep it away into the distant swimming bath. It bounced, I played my stroke, but the flight of the ball deceived me, and all I hit was air. The ball bounced up, struck me on the left shoulder and continued on its merry way in the direction of deep square leg.

I looked down the wicket at 'Cherry', who had a broad grin on his face. I smiled back at him. Then it happened. A squeaky boy-soprano voice rent the air: "Howzat?" I looked again at 'Cherry', his face now beaming with delight, and then – up went his hand. He had given me out! L.B.W! I think I can probably claim to be the only batsman ever given out 'leg before wicket' off his shoulder!

Then, just to add insult to injury, the heavens opened and flooded the pitch with torrential rain. Just two minutes earlier and I would have left the field with my reputation intact.

I think the effect that compulsory sport can have on a youngster was brought home to me most vividly when I made the acquaintance of the late Hector Bull. Hector and I were, I must confess, an ill-matched pair, though I derived much pleasure from his reminiscences of the earlier years of his life.

To begin with, Hector was several decades my senior – certainly quite old enough to have been my father and also to have experienced life in the very earliest years of this century. Then there was the manner of our upbringing. I have always regarded mine as having been a perfectly normal one; he felt the same about his, but the two were many poles apart.

Hector's father was in the Diplomatic Service and spent the greater part of his working life in British Embassies in distant capital cities all over the world. His wife invariably accompanied him on these postings, with the result that, though he was born in his grandfather's Manor House in the northern reaches of Norfolk, Hector was never destined to enjoy the solid foundation of a settled home. Indeed, in his early years he got to know his Nannie much better than his own mother, and then, as soon as possible, he was boarded out at a preparatory school until he was old enough to join his older brother at Eton. When holidays came round, he was not able to board a plane, as modern youngsters do, and jet off to whichever far-flung country was his parents' base at the time. It was a question of either descending upon relatives or, more frequently, accepting the hospitality offered by the parents of some schoolmate or other. This, to Hector, was "perfectly normal".

It was when he had done "two halves" at Eton (that's one year to us lesser mortals) that tragedy struck the family when Hector's brother died rather suddenly. Hector was just thirteen at the time and he and his brother had always been inseparable soulmates. Hence, it was decided that he should not return to Eton for the next "half", but should go with his parents to France, where his father was carrying out his duties in the British Embassy in Paris. It was thought to be a splendid opportunity for the youngster to learn French, but the plan was suddenly thwarted when his father was recalled to the Foreign Office in London. So, having no home of their own, the family went into lodgings in a small town in Kent.

The change in the family's circumstances, not surprisingly, did nothing to help the disconsolate Hector for, with Father going daily to the Foreign Office and Mother still mourning her lost son, he was left to his own devices in strange and friendless surroundings. He became steadily more disconsolate, and his father decided to take action. He had discovered that there was a private school in the town, kept by a chubby, smiling-faced clergyman with the very apt name of Mr. Kindleysides. Rather impulsively, but with the best of intent, he called at the school to ask whether his lonely son might join Mr. Kindleysides' boys for a game of football. "Yes indeed," said the reverend gentleman. "Let him report to the Games Master tomorrow and he can join the game".

Hector's father really should have been slightly less impulsive; he ought to have remembered his son's hatred of team games. When Hector had first entered Eton he had chosen to become a "wet-bob", with the avowed ambition of rowing in the College "Eight"; he was more than happy to leave football and cricket to the "dry-bobs". The coming encounter on the football field was destined to inflict on him an hour of such suffering and humiliation as would leave a scar for years.

His father, oblivious to any such thoughts, returned to their lodgings in fine fettle and announced the good news. Hector was horrified. He had never played football in his life and knew nothing of the rules of the game. He had seen Mr. Kindleysides' boys playing and had tried to work out what it was all about. There was all that intricate manoeuvring, then the curious periods of waiting about for something to happen, followed by the forward dash of some of the players, but all without any readily discernible pattern. He knew that it would be impossible for him, completely inexperienced, to walk on to that field and play football. He protested strongly, but his father swept all his objections aside.

"Not play football?" said his father. "A strong, active boy like you! Of course you can play football".

Hector tried another angle, pointing out that he had no football clothes – not even a pair of shorts.

"Shorts?" came the reply. "Only little boys wear shorts. You've got your knickerbockers and a jersey. And your brown boots will do perfectly!"

Further resistance would obviously be futile, so Hector resigned himself to a long night. Spiritless and overcome with panic, he lay on his bed and dreamily pictured the horror that the next day would bring. Then, as the fateful hour approached, he put on his grey flannel knickerbockers, his white jersey and his brown walking-boots with their slightly pointed toes. Then he walked – as slowly as he could – down to the school.

The little horrors with whom he was to play were already gathering together on the field, each one wearing shorts, stockings with coloured tops, and boots with strips of leather on the soles to save them from slipping. It was then, as he walked towards them, that he realised how small they were. He was a giant among pygmies, a Gulliver in Lilliput, but he was soon to learn that size was no substitute for skill.

The Games Master was readily identifiable, for he had a ball under his arm and a whistle on a piece of string around his neck. He wore a Norfolk jacket, an enormous woollen scarf and a look of utter healthiness. When Hector approached him, his face took on an expression of blank bewilderment, and it was patently clear that he had not been told of the lonely boy who had come for a game.

"Never mind," he said. "What position do you play in?"

Hector told him that he had never played football before, and the Games Master's bewildered look turned to one of incredulity.

"Never mind," he said once again. "You'll soon pick it up. I'll put you in Nobbler's side as an extra half-back".

Hector had no idea what a half-back might be, but he couldn't summon up the courage to ask. He soon identified Nobbler, for he was surrounded by his team, who obviously looked upon him with great reverence as their leader. Smaller than most of the others, he was a stocky little chap with a freckled face and an unruly mop of ginger hair. And it was he who was the main cause of Hector's humiliation for, in spite of his small stature, he was a footballing genius and dominated the entire proceedings.

"Well done, Nobbler!", "Well played, Nobbler!", "Shoot, Nobbler!". And Nobbler shot, and into the goal went the ball. On the few occasions when the ball came near Hector, he kicked it as hard as he could in the direction of the opposing goal, often destroying some well-planned move in the process, for he knew nothing of such subtleties as passing. Besides, most of the time he was unable to distinguish his team from the others and, as he blundered about, he became increasingly aware of his size, rather like a stick insect surrounded by a bustling group of ladybirds. And all the while there was Nobbler darting about and leaping in the air, tackling, intercepting, dribbling, passing and shooting, with the Games Master shouting approval from the touchline. What made it all the more painful was that the entire affair was carried out with an air of such utter seriousness. Oh, thought Hector, if only somebody would laugh! But football was clearly no laughing matter at Mr. Kindleysides' School. All around him there were serious, eagerly intent, contemptuous little faces. It was utter purgatory, and it went on for a full hour.

When, all those years later, he recounted the story, he had no recollection of having thanked his hosts for letting him play, nor of making any report to his father when he went back to the family lodgings. Perhaps his manner betrayed his emotions, for never again was it suggested that he should join the Kindleysides boys for another game.

Football was to remain Hector's *bête noire* for the rest of his life. He was happy to leave the game to others while he engaged in his "wet-bob" activities at Eton, in which he seems to have achieved more than a little success, for he was rowing in the College Eight by the time he was seventeen and went on to become Captain of the Boats. As regards cricket, of which he was a happy watcher but, to his regret, not the best of players, there were two counts on which he accused it of pretending to be something that it was not – and I confess to a degree of sympathy with him.

Firstly, there was its claim to be a "team game". How can a game involve genuine team-work, he asked, when during its whole course nine members of the batting side are sitting, impotent spectators, in the pavilion? While they sit in isolation, there are just two of their team out in the middle, each of them dependent upon nothing but his own skill and resolve. Then, as regards the fielders, though they can "back up" each other, a catch comes to a single pair of hands – the rest can only stand and pray. He had a point!

His main source of irritation, however, was the claim made by its devotees that cricket was the best of all "character builders" and the fact that any action carried out in anything less than the best of taste was denounced as being "not cricket". To begin with, there are the effects which the weather can have on the fortunes of the respective sides. Rain can save a side from defeat; a hot sun on a drying wicket can favour the bowlers unfairly. But, he asked, are these accidents which bring about victory or defeat in spite of the true merits of the sides deplored by cricketers? On the contrary, they are devoutly prayed for by those whose side they are likely to help.

Then there was that highly-regarded talisman of English cricket, Dr. W.G. Grace, remembered not only for his cricketing prowess but just as much for his wiles and ruses at the crease. If the stories that are told of the great man are true, his play was not always "cricket". It was left to a later generation and a certain Stephen Potter to find another name for it: gamesmanship. Then, of course, there was the time when the Australians were so upset by Harold Larwood's body-line bowling that they seemed to be on the verge of seceding from the British Empire.

I understand that, in more recent years, another tactic has been introduced into Test Cricket. They call it "sledging" and it is based on a threatening display of verbal intimidation directed at an incoming batsman by the close fielders. I am told that the Australians are very adept at it and that our own national team is not averse to bringing it into play at crucial times.

There was a time, however, when cricket was played by gentlemen in a gentlemanly manner. The turf on which they played was always "hallowed", and the whole affair was conducted with a degree of reverence which would not have been inappropriate in a place of worship. Above all, cricket demanded good manners and a high degree of decorum, and no team displayed those characteristics more wholeheartedly than I Zingari. Their name translates from the Italian as "The Gypsies", and that is what they were, for they travelled over various parts of the country, playing against local sides wherever they went. They were all, of course, dedicated amateurs, and it was a great cricketing honour to be admitted to the ranks of I Zingari. It was on one of their visits to

Somerset that Hector Bull, the confirmed "wet-bob" with no great cricketing talent, had one of his most memorable sporting experiences by actually playing for I Zingari.

There was a cricket week at Brympton, where Hector was staying with Tim Fane, one of his Eton friends, and the Brympton eleven were to play I Zingari. The visitors, however, found themselves short of two players, and Hector and Tim were roped in to make up the number. Forgetting his embarrassment with the Kindleysides boys, Hector played without a qualm in grey flannels and brown tennis shoes among the immaculate white trousers and even whiter cricket boots.

It had rained all night, but a hot sun came out and made the drying wicket exceedingly treacherous. I Zingari batted first and, one after the other, the talented cricketers were skittled out by the spin bowlers, albeit in the most stylish manner. Hector and Tim naturally batted last, and when, with nine men out, they came together at the wicket there were just fifty runs on the board. The two lads knew nothing about sticky wickets – they were delighted that they had slow bowlers to face. They charged down the pitch and slogged every ball. They ran between the wickets like scalded cats, and together they added over thirty runs to the score. Hector made twenty-two not out, the highest score of the innings.

The fielding side were disgusted. "This nonsense must stop," shouted one of them. Tim's father, keeping wicket for Brympton, looked decidedly haggard. Even their own side disapproved of their performance. Not a single clap did they get when they eventually returned together to the pavilion; not one word of congratulation was said to the beaming top-scorer. "Not cricket" was the general verdict. You see, the two lads had laughed and shouted as they ran, and generally upset the decorum of the most sacred of all games. But none of this could depress them, for they had taken no vows of submission to the rules.

"It was a glorious quarter of an hour," said Hector. "It would have been even more glorious if the captain of our side, so pained, so embarrassed, had been called Nobbler".

The thing I liked best about Hector Bull was his never-failing ability to see the funny side of life.

"How pleasant it is to grow up," he said. "To achieve some sort of athletic success; to develop a sense of humour; to be able to find fun in being a fish out of water".

What a splendid philosophy of life!

April 1st.

Prompo and Sugar-my-Sop.

I sometimes think that, if our grandparents were able to revisit the scene of their earlier time on earth, the most striking change they would notice might well be the aura of uniformity which exists in present-day society. Indeed, it is such that one sometimes begins to wonder whether we are, at last, in the first stages of the classless society which almost every Prime Minister since the War has promised us.

It shows itself in matters sartorial where, as in so many other aspects of present-day life, the transatlantic influence is well in evidence. How different it might have been if Mr. Levi had never introduced his jeans to an eager public. Yet, even in more formal attire, conformity has become the watchword. Looking back, I recall the days when, as callow youths, we yearned for adult status and for the one great acquisition which was synonymous with that state of life – a blue serge suit. Truly a modest enough yearning, but it was one of the major symbols which marked our entry into the state of manhood. Now, however, serge has become almost a thing of the past, its place in the world of fashion usurped by "man-made fibres", and blue also seems to be out of favour. There, in gents' outfitters' shops, modern suits can be seen, all in anonymous shades of grey, hanging limply in their hundreds from the rails in the ready-made department. Then, off they go, to hang – equally languidly in many cases – from the shoulders of all manner of men, from office workers to Ministers of the Crown. Conformity is truly the watchword.

Yet it is not only in the matter of dress that uniformity exists, for it can be found in the very people themselves. There is little doubt that they are greatly more knowledgeable than were the folk of my boyhood. This is by no means surprising, for Further Education is readily available to all, and University degrees, once the prerogative of the privileged few, are now obtainable from higher educational establishments in almost every city in the country. Yet, all these improvements in the lives of the people have not been achieved without cost. In bringing them about, we have lost something which, in earlier days, was revered as part of the very fabric of Norfolk life. I am referring to the many "characters" who went about their business among us – the eccentric and the unorthodox, the pathetic and, sometimes, the outrageous men and women in whose book the word "conformity" never existed.

There was, for example, "Blind Billy", existing in a world of darkness but endeavouring to earn a living by selling bootlaces at the Saturday Cattle Market. There was "Little Joe", with threadbare clothing and doleful expression, singing the one and only song in his repertoire, a pathetic offering made even more agonising by the lack-lustre quality of his performance. I cannot think that Billy and Joe would have performed in the city streets today – the Welfare State would have taken care of them. But I doubt whether even that commendable piece of legislation would have stopped "Billy Bluelight" from selling sprigs of heather by the Royal Arcade in summer or hawking cough sweets from door to door in the winter. He was too much of an independent character to expect other people to fight his battles for him.

All three of those men have already figured in previous books, but there were others whose memory I believe to be worthy of celebrating.

To begin with, there was "Prompo", whose calling was that of supplying the housewives of Norwich with linen line props, or promps as they were more correctly known in the Norfolk idiom – hence his nickname. He obtained his merchandise from various localities on the outskirts of the city where he knew that tree felling or coppicing was going on. He would select the longest and strongest, each with that forked branch at the top to hold the linen line as high as possible, and then he would trundle them round the city on his unwieldy handcart. He found a ready market for his wares, for there were no such things as drip-dry materials or spin-driers, and his customers, especially those living in the enclosed city yards, welcomed the means to project their washing skywards and to "give it a good blow".

In common with most of the other city "characters", Prompo suffered greatly at the hands of the local urchins. It was by no means an uncommon occurrence for him, having completed a sale, to return to his handcart to find his load of promps tipped out into the street. But he took it all as a matter of course. He simply loaded up again and set off.

He was a good businessman but, if popular legend is to be

Blind Billy, the bootlace vendor.

Beckwith Court, Norwich – typical of the congested areas where Prompo's linen promps were in demand. This court ran from the middle of Quayside and took its name from John Christmas Beckwith, organist at St. Peter Mancroft and the Cathedral.

believed, not always an entirely honest one. It is understandable that not all his promps were of the same quality. Some were quite naturally longer and stronger than the others, and it was those which he demonstrated to his prospective purchasers. Furthermore, it was those which he sold – but only on a temporary basis. Norwich at that time was not the city of eternal daylight which it has now become. When Nature decreed that darkness should fall, it duly fell, and it was then that he would venture out and surreptitiously substitute one of the more inferior promps, taking back the other for another day's trading. At least, that is the story that has been passed down through the years.

I have no knowledge of Prompo's real name, nor do I know the years in which he began and ended his stay on Earth. The only recorded detail is that he was born on April 1st, a fact which he always regretted, for the city boys were aware of it and never failed to come up with something extra special to mark the occasion. Under his door in the early morning would come a pencilled note ordering half a dozen promps to be delivered to a certain address. He would hastily select them and be on his way, for such an order was something not to be missed. Then, as he arrived at the delivery address, he would be met by the young perpetrators of the hoax, giving forth in unison with the chant of "April Fool, Prompo". Every year it was something different, but every year he was caught. But he could never avoid falling into the trap – after all, it might really be a bit of business!

The quaintly named "Sugar-my-Sop" was another of the band of Norwich eccentrics who suffered the taunts and abuse of the city's youngsters, and his torment was aggravated by similar treatment from his harridan of a wife. They lived in a modest house in Whalebone Square, opposite New Catton Church, and, though that was where they spent the greater part of their lives, their notoriety spread over the entire city.

Sugar-my-Sop's real name was William Potter, and he was said to have been born into a middle class family and to have received a good education. His main source of income, however, came from selling geraniums and other bedding plants, which he hawked around the city streets on a flat barrow mounted on penny-farthing cycle wheels. He and his wife were both of conspicuously tall stature, and they made a striking couple, he in his huge white apron, pulling the barrow while his spouse went from door to door

Sugar-my-Sop and his wife dressed for street entertaining.

soliciting custom.

They were an argumentative couple whose personal disagreements often spread out into the public arena. Yet they were deeply devoted to each other, and the memory is by no means simply that of just the eccentric man. She accompanied him on all his perambulations and is inseparable from his history. Wherever they went, come rain or sun, she invariably carried a parasol, but this was not to give protection from the weather, but rather to belabour her unfortunate spouse during their not infrequent public altercations. Yet she would defend him vigorously against outsiders, her only complaint being that he "used her face towel to wipe his feet on", a piece of information which she readily imparted to a large part of the population of Norwich.

When not engaged in supplying bedding plants to local householders, they would take themselves off along the city streets to present their own form of entertainment to passers-by. And they would dress themselves up for the purpose – he in his cutaway tailcoat and tall top hat with its green tinge acquired over the years, and she swathed from chin to ankles in exaggerated Victorian style, with scarves and an elaborate, flower-bedecked hat. Then, tapping time with one foot, he would play a lively burst of music on his accordion while his wife, with an expression of incongruous solemnity which never left her face, would cavort and pirouette in some form of Irish jig or similar dance.

They were, indeed, an odd couple, and it is not surprising that their activities should attract the jeering comments of some of the local urchins. The trouble was that they were both too quick-tempered to be able to ignore the youngsters' unwelcome attentions, and maledictions would rend the air in all directions. Then they would give chase, an action which was always doomed to fail, for both were inhibited in their movement – she by the length and tightness of her skirts, and Sugar-my-Sop by his peculiar crab-like gait and his great propensity for tripping over his walking stick.

Although Sugar-my-Sop was a contemporary of Billy Bluelight, surviving photographs of him and his wife are by no means as numerous as those of that other much-loved character. Indeed, I have only come across a single one which gives a clear impression of their physical features. The reason for this is probably because, whilst Billy delighted in posing for anybody with a camera, the reverse was the case with the odd couple. Unsolicited attempts to photograph them were greeted with a torrent of abuse and a distinct threat of physical assault. One man who succeeded in photographing them was T.M. Woods, proprietor of the Music Shop in Dove Street, who, after suffering abuse, was eventually invited to visit them at their home where, whilst he partook of tea and cakes, he was entertained by musical items from his host's accordion.

Much speculation has always surrounded the origin of Sugar-my-Sop's strange nickname, the most popular theory being that it arose from his habit, whilst engaged in his meticulous dressing routine, of shouting to his wife to "Sugar my sop". This may well be true but, if so, it must have been his mother to whom he was calling, for he acquired the name long before he was married.

His marriage, indeed, seems to be the only event in his life to which we can give an approximate date, for, as with Prompo,

Sugar-my-sop and his wife in more formal attire – surely the best photograph of the odd couple now in existence.

I know nothing of either his birth or death. It is thanks to Charles Barker, a former Norwich boy who emigrated to Canada, that we know the year to have been either 1903 or 1904. Young Charles was at that time a pupil at the old Higher Grade School in Duke Street, which had become the "Duke Street Municipal Secondary School", (now the Duke Street Centre).

One lunchtime, when turning from Duke Street into St. Andrew's, he came across a crowd of people around a small donkey cart in front of the Municipal Building, at the back of the Free Library. On enquiring the reason for the gathering, he was told that Sugar-my-Sop was inside getting married, so he decided to join the waiting throng. Eventually, out came the newly-married couple, who got into the donkey cart and drove away with the sound of the cheering crowd ringing in their ears.

Now, Sugar-my-Sop, like Prompo and all the others, is just a memory. The social history of old Norwich is liberally sprinkled with such people – but I fear we shall never see their like again.

Parson Woodforde's Health Hint.

April 11th, 1791: The Stiony on my right Eye-lid still swelled and inflamed very much. As it is commonly said that the Eye-lid being rubbed by the tail of a black Cat would do it much good if not entirely cure it, and having a black Cat, a little before dinner I made a trial of it, and very soon after dinner I found my Eye-lid much abated of the swelling and almost free from Pain. I cannot therefore but conclude it to be of the greatest service to a Stiony on the Eye-lid. Any other Cat's Tail may have the above effect in all probability, but I did my Eye-lid with my own black Tom Cat's Tail.

The Rev. James Woodforde,
The Diary of a Country Parson.

April 15th.

A Host of Golden Daffodils.

On the 15th of April in the year 1802, William Wordsworth and his sister Dorothy went walking near Grasmere in their beloved Lake District. Both were prolific writers but, whereas William's métier was verse, his sister's preference was for the prose with which she recorded in her *Journal* the sights and happenings of her everyday life. Having returned from their walk, it was Dorothy who immediately sat down to relate the details of what they had seen:

"When we were in the woods beyond Gowbarrow Park we saw a few daffodils close to the waterside. We fancied that the lake had floated the seeds ashore, and that the little colony had so sprung up. But as we went along there were more and yet more; and at last, under the boughs of the trees, we saw that there was a long belt of them along the shore, about the breadth of a country turnpike road".

The sudden sight of a swathe of golden daffodils never fails to stir emotions, and many writers have been moved to translate those emotions into words. Few, however, have portrayed them as vividly as did Dorothy Wordsworth in her *Journal:*

"I never saw daffodils so beautiful. They grew among the mossy stones around and about them; some rested their heads upon those stones as on a pillow for weariness; and the rest tossed and reeled and danced, and it seemed as if they verily laughed with the wind... they looked so gay, ever glancing, ever changing".

Then, lest their beauty should be forgotten, she pressed some of their blooms and placed them within the pages of her *Journal.*

Unlike his sister, William wrote nothing when they returned from their walk. Instead, he made straight for his bookshelves to select something to read. "He brought out," said Dorothy, "a volume of Enfield's *Speaker,* another miscellany, and an odd volume of Congreve's plays". That, it seems, was the end of the matter. Dorothy had recorded her prose, but from William there came not a single line of verse.

It was to be two years later that, quite by chance, he came upon the faded blooms which his sister had lovingly pressed between the pages of her *Journal*. The memory of their walk near Grasmere came instantly back into his mind and he sat for a time in silent recollection. Then, taking up his pen, he painted, in words, the picture of that waterside walk and the daffodils near Gowbarrow Park:

Continuous as the stars that shine
And twinkle on the milky way,
They stretched in never-ending line
About the margin of a bay:
Ten thousand saw I at a glance,
Tossing their heads in sprightly dance.

Now, why should I choose to write of the Wordsworths in a diary of Norfolk happenings? It is, simply, that William's splendid poem sprang instantly into my mind when reading of the travels of William Turner, the Tudor botanist. He was a man who journeyed widely in search of flowering plants and, whenever he discovered one, he made great efforts to find out the name by which it was known to the locals. When travelling in Norfolk, however, as with many a visitor in earlier times, he did not always find information easy to acquire. The flower that attracted him when he was in our county was not the golden daffodil, but a very close relative, the virginal white narcissus. But what was it called?

"When I was taking a holiday in Norfolk," he wrote, "a little girl hardly seven years old met me as I was walking along the road; she was carrying in her right hand a bunch of white flowers; as soon as I saw them I thought to myself, 'those are Narcissi', but when I inquired the name no reply was forthcoming. So I asked the folk who lived in the neighbouring cottages and villages, what was the name of the plant. They all answered that it was called *laus tibi:* I could get no other name from them".

What a splendidly romantic lot our ancestors must have been, for, if my schoolboy Latin does not let me down, *laus tibi* translates as 'Praise be to thee'. What a delightful name for any flower – and, of course, there are many others peculiar to our county.

The wild arum is known by a variety of names such as 'cuckoo pint' and 'Lords and Ladies', but only in Norfolk have I heard it called, so appropriately, 'Parson in the Pulpit'. Then there is Astrantia, aptly known in Suffolk as 'Polly's Pincushion', but in

Astrantia.

Herb Robert.

the depths of Norfolk most mysteriously given the name of 'Melancholy Gentleman'.

There are exceptions, of course, for if countryfolk found that a certain plant, when bruised, gave off an unpleasant odour, they immediately gave it a prefix to indicate their displeasure, which gives us 'stinking iris', 'stinking hellebore' and a host of others. There is even the delightful little wild geranium, Herb Robert, about which Wordsworth himself wrote:

Poor Robin is yet flowerless, but how gay
With his red stalks upon this sunny day.

But the countryman's·name? None other than 'Stinking Bob'.

I find this hurtful, for it is a little plant of which I am rather fond. Much more worthy, I feel, of the title *laus tibi*.

May 19th

The School Magazine.

On more than one occasion I have heard it said that poetry is the most snobbish form of artistic expression. This, of course, is a dangerous generalisation for, though there are times when some pieces of poetic work achieve a kind of cult-like status of which they are by no means worthy, the weaving of words by somebody with genuine talent for his art can produce a picture every bit as enchanting as though it were in paint upon a canvas.

Having said that, I can state without fear of contradiction that there was nothing snobbish about the poetic work which we boys churned out in our Council School days. Harry Allen had joined the staff as the new English master, and it was he who stimulated our interest in this new literary form of expression. We rather liked it, and we steadily set about producing masterpieces. Three of us, indeed, formed ourselves into a select group known as "The Busy

Bs" – the reason there were just three of us was that we were the only ones whose surnames began with the letter B. Before long, however, we opened up membership to other boys who shared our interest in versifying, and thus was born "The North Walsham Society of Poets". Lest this should sound both precocious and presumptuous, I hasten to add that we were only ten years old at the time – and the N.W.S.P. had a very short life.

In recent years I have discovered the whereabouts of surviving members, now widely spread around the globe, but not one of them can recall any memories of that poetic band. I am the fortunate one, however, for it was into my safe keeping that all the original manuscripts were entrusted when, in 1932, we left the Council School and went our various ways.

As I now browse through them, it becomes patently clear that, apart from our rather modest degree of talent, we had one other handicap – our insatiable sense of humour. In the years that have followed, there have been many occasions when I have had cause to thank my Maker for endowing me with that precious gift, but it was something of a hindrance when we were endeavouring to produce work of a serious nature. All the splendid flowing phrases were there, but I have a strong suspicion that, if such men as Walter De La Mare and Messrs. Keats, Shelley and Wordsworth were able to read them, they would probably detect a slightly familiar ring about them.

No, it has to be said that our great strength lay in our Nonsense Verse. This sort of thing:

> *'Twas on an April morning*
> *In December last July;*
> *The sun was falling lightly*
> *And the snow shone in the sky;*
> *The cow was sitting in the tree,*
> *The blackbird chewed the cud;*
> *The frog was making honey*
> *And the bee was eating mud;*
> *The flowers were singing gaily,*
> *The birds were in full bloom,*
> *As I went down in my cellar*
> *To sweep the upstairs room.*

Like all schoolboys, we delighted in putting new words to well-known pieces of work, as in our 1930 version of *The Village Smithy:*

Under the spreading chestnut tree the village smithy stands
Behind a row of petrol pumps of all the well-known brands,
Where greasy men with oily grins take money
with both hands.
Week in, week out, from morn till night,
your empty tank they'll fill;
They'll change a tyre or turn a nut with plenty of goodwill;
But all the same you'll later find it's all down on the bill.

Perhaps I may be forgiven for including just one more piece, which, I seem to recall, was very much a joint effort, and which bore the title: *The Intruder.*

A Beecham's Pill came rolling, into a cemetery,
And round and round the tombstones it rolled so merrily.
The noise woke up a skeleton who'd lain beneath the moss,
And now at last, its rest disturbed, awakened very cross.
So it shouted at the Beecham's, "No need to make this fuss;
Please don't hang around this place –
you'll get nothing out of us!"

Eventually there came the Scholarship Examination, with those of us who found favour in the eyes of the examiners passing on to the Grammar School. There, of course, we were in a different league, with much greater demands being made on our literary skills. Those demands, furthermore, came at us from two different directions.

First of all there was the English master introducing us to a kind of poetry we had never before encountered. The lines were of greatly differing lengths, they did not rhyme and, as far as we could make out, they did not even scan. It was our first meeting with William Shakespeare, and it was not a happy one. We felt at home with the rhyme and rhythm of such as Chesterton, Kipling and Brooke, but having to learn by heart great chunks of verse without understanding what it all meant was not the easiest of tasks. Perhaps we were unfortunate in having Julius Caesar as our introduction to the Bard; by the time we reached his *Silvia,* and especially his

... daisies pied and violets blue,
And lady-smocks all silver-white,
And cuckoo-buds of yellow hue
Do paint the meadows with delight

we were happy to declare a truce, so much so that I can still remember the pieces we learnt from *As You Like It,* our 'set-book' for the 1936 School Certificate.

But, as I have said, there was another quarter from which our literary skills were sorely tested, and that was the School Magazine. Being editor of *The Pastonian* must, at times, have been a thankless task, for the wearer of that mantle was required to fill, by fair means or foul, the decreed number of pages. It is true that much of it was readily available to him but, when he had collected together the House Reports, the Cricket or Football Results, the list of School Officials, the Cadet Corps Report and all the other regular items, he was inevitably left with quite a number of blank pages to fill. It was then that he went in search of likely boys whom he could either cajole or coerce into helping to fill the void. Needless to say, most of us, at some time or other, succumbed to his blandishments.

I recently climbed the ladder into my loft and, from a dark corner, retrieved some two dozen copies of *The Pastonian* covering the years when my three brothers and I had been at the School, and brought them out into the daylight for the first time in half a century. Now, having read their contents, I can only express my gratitude both to the writers and to the editors who gathered the pieces together, for there is much within them to savour.

In accordance with tradition, the writers were always identified simply by their initials, which hardly carried any great degree of anonymity. Amongst the items of prose there were two which particularly took my fancy, one being a dramatic tale penned in 1929 by F.I.C. – readily identifiable as F.I. Childs, Prefect and Captain of Wharton House:

The silence of the night had fallen. Stealthily he crept from the hiding place where he had lain so long with cramped limbs, and furtively looked about him. The coast was clear, and he made his way quietly over the stone floor, dragging himself slowly forward on all fours and scarcely daring to breathe. On both sides were great, high, inaccessible galleries projecting from the wall in tiers one above the other, and here were valuables of all kinds. But still he went on, steadily, silently, past great cages where the wild beasts were already dead, towards the end of the vast hall. There, on a wooden dais, lay the treasure he sought, gleaming dully in the faint light.

How he longed for it, how often he had admired it! How fine and alluring it looked now when almost within his reach! Eagerly he rushed forward, seized it and turned to go. Suddenly he staggered back. There came a swift rush of wind. A black shape flashed down in the dim light and crashed to the floor. Half stunned, he reeled breathless a moment, and then dashed off with all the speed of fear. Again he had gambled with Death and won.

Next morning a man opened the pantry door and said, "We've missed that mouse again, my dear, but the cheese has gone".

The second piece of prose was written in 1927 by S.B. – none other than my older brother Stanley. I chose it purely on merit, for I believe it shows, even at the age of fourteen, a promise of the talent which, in later years, was to shine so brightly over the local journalistic scene:

William – a Sewerage Aristocrat.

It was obvious at a glance that he was something out of the ordinary, something above the common run of sewerage workmen. Yet he was dressed no better than the remainder, his personal appearance was neither commanding nor dignified, and altogether it seemed difficult to give any reason for this distinction.

It certainly could not have been his appearance! His face had none of the characteristics of a Wellington or a Napoleon, and was, in fact, considerably more inclined to be homely than handsome, jovial than severe. His shirt was most notable by its insignificance, his trousers defied description, and his belt, unable entirely to surround the extraordinary rotundity of his waist, was manfully doing its best around the top of his legs.

He mixed quite freely with the rest, chewed his dinner even more heartily, and evidently considered himself not at all superior to his fellow workmen. Indeed, at such times he did not appear so, for the difference only became apparent during <u>working</u> hours.

It was all a question of superiority in art – the

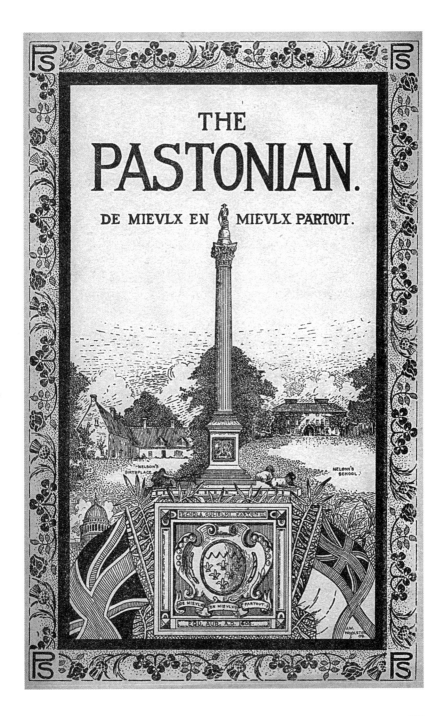

THE
PASTONIAN.

DE MIEVLX EN MIEVLX PARTOUT.

difference between a Rembrandt and a dabbler in water colours. Only in this case the art lay in the avoiding of work. The others might stealthily follow the movements of the foreman, taking advantage of any temporary absence to relax their efforts, but with William it was different. He did not so much avoid work as become totally oblivious of it. The laziness or late arrival of the others might call forth a stream of epithets and vituperations; but William calmly turned up half an hour late, and went off at once into a trance which lasted until dinner-time.

As time went on he became almost an institution, as regular as School itself. It might be that, all this time, matters of international importance were revolving and rotating in his brain, something perchance that was to startle the world and revolutionise its industries. Perhaps he was standing and thinking of unbelievable constructions and astounding discoveries; or perhaps, on the other hand, he was merely standing.

But one sad evening this tradition of a term's duration was broken. It was after a month's holiday that I discovered the miracle that had taken place. Something during those few weeks must have upset all his ideals, changed him from something apart to a mere nonentity like the rest.

For William was working! Working vigorously, beating a carpet in a small back garden. The proud spirit that had withstood for so long the wrath, the scorn, and the sarcasm of generations of foremen, had been broken at last by the insidious misrepresentations of a female.

William had got married!

There is another piece of writing which, I believe, is worthy of note, not because of any literary merit, but rather on account of its historical interest. It appeared in the editorial notes of the Summer issue of 1926, produced jointly by F.A. Gillion and A.T. Standley.

"Like everyone else," they wrote, "the School has suffered inconvenience through the unfortunate General Strike at the beginning of the term. Some of us were obliged to cycle long distances to School; a few keen scholars walked anything up to

"S.B."

ten miles, setting off very early in the morning, and a small number were unable to attend School at all. We are still handicapped by a lack of trains and do not get home until sometimes 9 p.m."

The Pastonian always carried poetry in profusion, with something to appeal to all tastes. In 1930 R.W. delved into the realms of classical romanticism with his piece, *To Helen:*

> *Helen, thy beauty is to me*
> *Far dearer than that maid of yore*
> *Whose loveliness across the sea*
> *Drew Grecian heroes unto war,*
> *And made them leave their well-loved native shore.*
>
> *Long years have passed since that fair girl*
> *Did live and cause men's hearts to burn*
> *With love, and set their minds awhirl,*
> *But still do maids men's hearts o'erturn,*
> *And so my love to you do I unfurl.*
>
> *When first I saw thy beauteous face*
> *I vowed I'd seek to make thee mine;*
> *I sought, and now my heart I place*
> *At thy fair feet as at a shrine,*
> *For you to throw aside or to embrace.*

There was an understandable lack of romanticism about W.H.H. as he recorded the arrival of an unwelcome annual visitor:

> *The Dentist.*
>
> *I am king of the van I survey;*
> *My might is right, and forsooth!*
> *From the van all round the School yard*
> *I am lord of the boy and his tooth.*
> *Oh! Jimmy, where are those teeth gone*
> *That I formerly saw in your face?*
> *You would rather dwell in the midst of alarms*
> *Than visit my horrible place.*

There came an occasion when a group of us, fourth formers all, were approached by a desperate editor with a multitude of pages that needed filling. There was more than a hint of flattery as he beseeched our help, and we were unable to resist his pleadings. The big difficulty, however, was finding a subject. What we needed was a source of inspiration, but such things were in rather short supply in the everyday routine of classroom life. Eventually, however, we had a bright idea – we would write about our school museum!

At this point I must make it clear that the museum in question was not the collection of Nelson memorabilia displayed in School House and greatly revered by all. The subject of our attention was to be a lesser assortment of objects, veering towards natural history and displayed in our own classroom, Form IVa. There, fixed to the wall above the lockers, was a collection of animal exhibits – the skull of a lion and another of a bear, a complete crocodile and an armadillo, heads bearing horns in a great variety of forms – all gazing down upon us as we went through our daily tribulations:

> *Just step inside and look around*
> *And keep your glance above the ground,*
> *And on the walls, hung up, you'll see*
> *What seem like curios, maybe:*
> *A lion's skull of monstrous size,*
> *With ugly holes which were the eyes;*
> *Then near to this on either side*
> *Hang two more skulls securely tied,*
> *One a dingo, one a bear,*
> *Though which is which I cannot swear.*
> *But really worse than all of those,*
> *So we've been told by one who knows,*
> *Are those queer fossils which we find*
> *Sitting at desks with vacant mind.*

That piece had earlier appeared in *The Pastonian*, but we were not content to leave it at that, for we had rather rebellious feelings about "our" museum. The specimens had come from a variety of sources, in many cases from Old Boys who had ventured far across the globe. It was the heyday of the British Empire and, though many Old Pastonians stayed loyal to their county roots, others went off to seek their fortunes in the many far-flung countries which were then coloured pink on the Map of the World.

It was the iguana which focussed our minds on the matter, for it had been given to the School in 1927 by a certain Mrs. Spinks, with the information that her husband had shot it in the Malay States. There were those among us who felt the time had come to make our peace with the iguana – and all the other specimens that adorned the wall of our Form Room. There followed many hours of frantic soul-searching, and then the feeling of blissful reconciliation as the words fell into place:

Ode to an Iguana.

I've never seen the Amazon,
I've never reached Brazil;
But I've seen an iguana,
Though I never had until
Someone perched it o'er the lockers,
And decreed that it must stay
To ornament and decorate
Our classroom, Form IVa.

When he hunted in the forest
And devoured a captured meal,
Or another creature's dinner
Most craftily did steal,
Did he think a hunter'd kill him
And carry him away
To ornament and decorate
Our classroom, Form IVa?

Oh, the poor old iguana,
Did he ever wish to be
Mounted up above the lockers
For everyone to see?
He'd have pined away, poor fellow,
If he'd known he'd have to stay
To ornament and decorate
Our classroom, Form IVa.

Finally, whilst praising the many boys who, over the years, brought the pages of the School Magazine to life, here is a piece which surely echoes the sentiments of all who, from 1606 onwards, walked within the walls of Paston. The author was C. Poll, Boarder, Prefect and Captain of Wharton House, and it was written before breakfast on the morning of May 19th, 1926:

Memories.

> *Some six long years have passed away*
>   *Since first I came to School,*
> *A funny little chap about*
>   *The height of yonder stool.*
> *Ten more weeks and I must leave,*
>   *This term will be my last,*
> *How everything in this old room*
>   *Reminds me of the past.*
>
> *The big boys were so very big*
>   *And mighty in my eyes,*
> *But they've been dwindling ever since,*
>   *At least in point of size;*
> *It's not so unaccountable,*
>   *Considering how I've grown,*
> *And now, a prefect of the School,*
>   *I'm sitting here alone.*
>
> *The masters too – Hallo, what's that?*
>   *Exactly what I thought;*
> *The breakfast bell is ringing;*
>   *So I'll cut these verses short,*
> *With "Long live the Paston Boys!*
>   *The Masters long live they!"*
> *The enjoyment that I've had at School*
>   *Can I e'er again repay?*

Yarmouth Disasters.

It was on a day in May in 1845 that the people of Yarmouth were stunned by the greatest disaster in the town's history, and it came about as the result of a publicity stunt that went terribly wrong.

Cooke's Equestrian Circus was in town, and that fact alone was sufficient to raise the minds of the populace to a high degree of expectancy. Then the mood became one of euphoria when it was announced that Nelson, one of the clowns, was to sail down the River Bure from the old Drawbridge to the Suspension Bridge in a wash-tub pulled by a team of geese! The effect of this news on the townsfolk, not surprisingly, was magnetic and, by the time the novel feat was to be undertaken, a crowd of many thousands had congregated in the area, with as many as four or five hundred spectators packed on to the Suspension Bridge itself.

Then, as the clown in his strange craft came into view, the atmosphere became electric, and it was then that the tragedy occurred. The watchers on the bridge, in order to miss nothing of the scene, immediately surged across from the northern side to that on the south, with disastrous results. The sudden transfer of such a large weight from one side to the other caused the suspension rods to snap and the chains to give way. In the words of the local Press reporter, "the bridge fell on that side like letting down the leaf of a table" and threw the spectators into the water.

It was a horrific sight, with the waters of the Bure becoming full of struggling, terrified people. Rescuers immediately set to work, with local boatmen bringing as many as possible back to the shore to be tended at the Vauxhall Gardens. In spite of their efforts, however, the tremendous scale of the tragedy became apparent when it was known that 77 people had lost their lives. Even more tragic, perhaps, was the fact that most of the victims were young people and children, with an even greater number injured.

At the inquest which followed, Mr. Cooke, the circus proprietor, expressed his deep sorrow at the tragic accident and intimated that he would at once withdraw his company from the town.

At the subsequent inquiry, the findings of experts declared that the causes of the tragedy were threefold. The immediate factor was a defect in the welding of the bar which first gave way; the quality of the iron and the workmanship was also below standard; and, in the original construction of the bridge, the effect of such a heavy load all on one side did not appear to have been contemplated.

Eighteen years later, another tragedy, though on a somewhat smaller scale, was reported in the *Norfolk News* of May 30th, 1863:

On Wednesday afternoon the Deputy Coroner (C. Diver Esq.) held an inquest at the Yarmouth Workhouse on the body of a man named Charles Marsh, who had met with his death on the previous afternoon by falling from the top of the Nelson Monument, South Denes. The deceased was a professional singer and acrobat, and for some time past had fulfilled engagements as such at the Theatre and various public places of resort in the town.

On Tuesday afternoon he and a "pal" named Henry Warton dressed themselves up as "niggers", and with a violin and banjo went on to the South Denes in the hope of earning a trifle by amusing the folk who had assembled there for the purpose of enjoying the Whitsuntide holidays. It would seem they were not very successful in drawing coppers from the pockets of these persons into their own, and accordingly, after having refreshed themselves at the tavern there situate, they for their own amusement ascended the monument.

At the top, Warton amused himself by looking through the telescope there provided, and while so engaged, his companion, from, it is presumed, a love of dangerous exploits, and a desire to show his skill as an acrobat, climbed upon one of the caryatides, and from thence to the figure of Britannia, which is placed at the very top. Upon the shoulders of Britannia he performed various feats, and then endeavoured to descend, but he missed the trident and lightning rod by which he had mounted, and fell with a terrific crash to the ground beneath, a distance of 144 feet.

There is no doubt it was a pure accident, and the jury returned a verdict in accordance with these circumstances.

Henry Blogg.

Fifty years he faced the storms
That lash the grim North Sea;
And where the gale raged fiercest
His boat was bound to be.
There came no call unanswered
From seamen in distress;
He said it was his duty,
And he could do no less.

With knowledge, skill and courage
He led that gallant band,
Who saved a thousand seamen
From storm and shoal and sand;
Till, full of years and honour,
He stood upon the land
And watched The Boat plough seaward,
Steered by a younger hand.

He has sailed to his last haven,
Upon the ageless shore,
Where the sea is ever peaceful
And shipwrecks are no more.
He has gone from Cromer beach,
Washed by the North Sea swell,
But his name will live forever
With us, who knew him well.

W.J. Mayes.

Henry Blogg, G.C., B.E.M.

Henry Blogg served aboard the Cromer Lifeboat for 53 years, 38 of them as coxswain. During that time, the Boat put to sea on 387 occasions, saving 873 human lives and a dog. He became the most highly decorated of all lifeboatmen, being awarded the George Cross and the British Empire Medal by his Country and receiving the Gold Medal of the R.N.L.I. three times and the Silver Medal on four occasions. He retired from the Boat in 1947, to be succeeded as coxswain by his nephew, Henry "Shrimp" Davies. He died on the evening of Sunday, June 13th, 1954.

June 19th.

The Silver Spoon.

I have often thought that I have much for which to thank my Maker, not least the fact that I did not make my entry into the world with a silver spoon in my mouth. I was born into what I can only describe as a normal, conventional family, with three elder brothers and a couple of parents who worked hard but were always on hand when we needed them. We were very much a self-contained unit with – to borrow a seafaring analogy – Father as skipper and Mother as navigator. Furthermore, I have always believed myself to be the most fortunate member of the family, for we are told nowadays that every child needs a 'role model' to influence its development, and I had five of them. I know full well that, deep within me, there is a little bit of each of them. Yet, how different it might have been if Fate had not decreed that Doctor Grant should aid my entry into the world, all those years ago, in that bay-windowed bedroom above the old Press Office in Cromer.

These thoughts were never far from my mind as I ambled through the various reminiscences of the late Sir Lawrence Jones, for it was he, unlike me, who had the silver spoon. Indeed it would be true to say that the only common factor in our lives was a shared birthday, and, even then, there was more than a generation between us. Queen Victoria was on the throne and the nineteenth century still had more than a decade to run when he made his entry into the world at Cranmer Hall, three miles from Fakenham and "a third of a mile from the high-road, in turnip-land; a country of scattered farms and cottages, badly served by railways, and turning an indifferent face towards strangers". His father was the latest in a long line of Joneses to inherit the squirearchy, together with the baronetcy bestowed upon one of his earlier illustrious predecessors. Their portraits glowed from the walls of the Entrance Hall – Sir John, whose letters from the Duke of Wellington were preserved in the glass-topped treasure table in the drawing-room, together with a lock of Napoleon's hair; Sir Harry, who had distinguished himself in both the Peninsular and Crimean Wars; and Captain George, R.N.

Cranmer Hall.

But it was to be some years before young Lawrence was likely to take any sort of interest in those splendid family portraits. First, there was the serious business of infancy to be tackled, and it was at this point in his narrative that I gladly conceded him the silver spoon:

"During his first four or five years," he wrote, "the child of a country squire in the reign of Queen Victoria spent nine-tenths, if not more, of his waking hours in the company of servants. It was from them that he learnt the intricate business of eating, washing, dressing and 'behaving', with all their imposed rituals, and it was to them that his natural affections first turned".

Foremost among those surrogate parents must surely have been the Nanny, although, somewhat surprisingly, memories of her were the most difficult of all to recapture when, in his latter years, Lawrence Jones tried to recall his nursery days. He fondly remembered their own Emma Turner's reputation as a splendid 'bringer-up' of children, but his recollections of her as a physical entity were limited to misty visions of her, sitting by the nursery fire, rendering such varied musical offerings as "Just a Song at Twilight" and a heart-rending Victorian tear-jerker with words that went thus:

The fire has gone out,
The house is quite dark,
And Mother is sitting alone,
With poor brother Ben so sick on her lap,
Oh father, dear father, come home!

But, if the memory of Emma Turner had become lost in the inner recesses of his mind, the same could not be said of Ethel, a fourteen-year-old girl who came from the village as a temporary nursery-maid. Ethel was, to the very young Lawrence, "a heroine, an ideal" – a role model, in fact, for he longed to grow up to be like her. She was the very epitome of all those sweetly-appealing young girls to be seen in so many old Victorian paintings – her long, fair hair tumbling down to her shoulders, and the hem of her skirts stopping just sufficiently short to reveal a pair of hefty, black lace-up boots. But, above all, she had a languid air which tugged mercilessly at the little boy's heart-strings.

Ethel would lean against the nursery wall and cross one leg over the other, with only the toe of the crossed leg resting on the ground. Whilst taking up this posture, she radiated an aura of almost regal unconcernedness, and he longed to imitate her. His great handicap at the time, however, was his short, chubby legs, and when he tried to cross them as she did he merely succeeded in falling over. He resigned himself to looking forward to the day when, as he confided to the other maids, he would grow up to have long, fair hair and big lace-up boots and be called Ethel. He was still too young to have any knowledge of gender and thought he could grow up to be either a man or a woman. It was the sight of Ethel leaning against the wall with such utter nonchalance that made up his mind – he "wanted to be both beautiful and lordly".

There was another member of the nursery staff who lingered long in Lawrence's memory, and that was Nelly Bayliss, who became second nurse under Emma Turner. Unlike most of the other nursery-maids who, whatever their real names might be, were invariably called Alice, Nelly was always known by her real name, and she was much-loved by the children for a very understandable reason – she would stand no nonsense from them, but she was, above all, a 'sport'. At one end of the day nursery there was a raised mahogany platform which had, in grandfather's time, supported a bath, and, when the parents were away on one of their frequent visits to France or Switzerland, Nelly would climb up onto this vantage point and display her talent as an entertainer. Dressed in a pair of trousers borrowed from the footman, she would sing, dance and play the concertina. She could dance a very nautical hornpipe, and her songs covered a wide range from "The Roast Beef of Old England" to an un-named ditty which began thus:

The Prince of Wales was Chairman,
Of course he opened the Ball,
And sang the chorus of every song
In the Concert at Albert Hall.

Much of the children's enjoyment of Nelly's performance stemmed from the fact that it was all a secret they shared with her. Their parents were never told, for they knew Mother would not approve of Nelly in trousers.

Another great thing about Nelly Bayliss was that she had an aunt at Little Walsingham with whom they would sometimes take tea.

They never liked riding in the pony cart, but it was worth it to go and see Nelly's aunt in her cottage amongst the ruins of an ancient friary, with little stone staircases that led to nowhere in particular; and to see if she was still wearing the large black bonnet which seemed to be such a permanent fixture on her head.

There were times when even the drive to Walsingham was exciting, for a small diversion would take them through the leafy tunnel of Chestnut Grove at West Barsham, at the end of which they would pull up to watch the blacksmith at his anvil. Then there was the Slipper Chapel, where the pilgrims used to leave their shoes behind and walk the last mile barefoot. It was there that Nelly habitually repeated the old story of the two pilgrims who, for a penance, had to walk to Walsingham with peas in their boots. One hobbled along in great distress, but the other strode ahead without a care in the world – he had boiled the peas before stuffing them into his shoes. They never tired of hearing about such a master stroke.

Nelly also had another relative in the area, a lady known to the children simply as Mrs. Colman, but a visit to her could only take place when the parents were abroad, for it meant cajoling Coachman into driving them the fifteen miles to Gayton. That, however, was not as infrequent as one might have thought, for Doctor Kidd, by whose prognostications the parents set great store, had a marked tendency to recommend a few weeks in Schwalbach or Mentone or some other European resort. "Change of air – different scenery – do you more good than a bottle of medicine". They were ever ready to act upon his advice, and an unaccustomed air of freedom would settle over Cranmer.

Mrs. Colman was an outstanding hostess – in more ways than one! Physically, she was the fattest woman Lawrence had ever seen, and her kitchen table had a large half-circle cut out of one side, so that she could approach the food more closely at mealtimes. In reality, anything in front of her was still as far away as ever, but she was able to spread herself more freely and gain easier access to anything on either side.

The outstanding feature of teatime at Mrs. Colman's was the cream – a vast bowl of the stuff, and so rich and stiff that a spoon would readily stand up in it unaided. Furthermore, incredibly generous quantities of the tempting delicacy were shovelled out onto scones already well-laden with blackberry jam or crabapple jelly. Then there was the one rule which she strictly enforced with all her visitors – they must eat until they were 'full up'. The boys needed no encouragement, and it was at Mrs. Colman's that they first learnt the meaning of the word 'replete'. Then, as they left the table, there was nothing for it but a general unbuckling of belts and an admission that nowhere else had they ever been treated to such a magnificent meal.

There was one other great object of interest when they visited dear, jolly Mrs. Colman, and that was her outdoor privy. Now, this was a subject which they were not allowed to discuss back at the Hall, except perhaps in hushed whispers. At Mrs. Colman's however, tucked away behind the hollyhocks, there was a whole new world of interest, for it was a genuine three-holer, with each hole of different size as though it had been made for the Three Bears. At Mrs. Colman's it soon became apparent that one man's secret necessity was another man's social occasion.

Though the young Jones children had so little contact with their true parents, the staff at Cranmer Hall were sufficiently numerous to offer plenty of substitutes, sometimes with confusing results. In the housekeeper's room, Lawrence was Mrs. Annell's "little lamb" and was plied with pink finger biscuits, but in the stable-yard he was Coachman's "little lamb" as well, a joint ownership which puzzled him until Mrs. Annell's sudden overnight departure from the Hall. Because she always dressed in black and wore a huge lace cap with ribbons, Lawrence believed her to be very old. It was not until many years later that he learned that she was much younger than he thought – young enough, in fact, to have been discovered "in a compromising situation" with one of the butlers. Hence her sudden unannounced departure for Fakenham Station and the first available train back to her native Scotland. Henceforth, Coachman was to have undisputed ownership of his little lamb, although that ownership was not readily accepted by the little lamb himself.

To begin with, Coachman steadfastly refused to tell the children why he wore a cockade on the side of his top hat, and this was a source of great annoyance to them all. Then there was the presence in the stable-yard of a young man who, for a special reason, aroused strong feelings of hero-worship in Lawrence's mind. This was Jim, the groom, and it was his forearms that did the trick. As he sat cleaning harness, they were a source of great fascination, for, not only were they deep brown in colour, but they also bore a copious covering of little black hairs. This, said the maids, was because he was so strong. Another manservant had beads of perspiration on his forehead when he loaded up the baggage cart with portmanteaux for the annual holiday at Cromer. This, said the maids, was because he was NOT strong. Thus Jim was the man to join Lawrence's band of heroes.

This was not the case, however, with Mr. Basham, the Third Gardener. The children were fond of him, for he was a very affable man. He was also a rather large man and, when he bent down to do his weeding, which seemed to be his lifetime crusade, his prominent and well-rounded hindquarters stuck out behind him in a pretty fair imitation of those of Boxer and Smart, the carthorses at the Home Farm. It was when he stood upright to go to dinner, however, that doubts rose in Lawrence's mind for, though well-bearded, Mr. Basham had a clean-shaven upper lip, just as Lawrence's grandfather had in the portrait hanging in the Hall. Lawrence had been born too late to know his grandfather, and he never knew whether he ought to be proud of him, but it seemed inappropriate for the Third Gardener to share that shaven upper lip with the former Squire.

He had come by the baronetcy in November 1845 through the action of a Turkish bandit, who shot his elder brother (another Sir Lawrence) from behind a rock "at a distance of about three yards". He was riding through Turkey with his friend, Captain Richard Twopeny of the 52nd Regiment, together with a priest and his servant, when they spotted bandits skulking among some bushes ahead of them. Captain Twopeny was in favour of an attack on the bandits, but Sir Lawrence disagreed.

"We may as well have our lunch first," he said. "If these fellows mean to attack us, we can't escape them; and it is better to fight on a full stomach than an empty one".

Twenty minutes later, Jones and the servant were dead, the priest disarmed and Captain Twopeny wounded by "a shot in the left breast and a volley of thirteen slugs, six in the head and seven in the body". The bandits, having rifled their baggage, made off, and the priest managed to get Captain Twopeny across a horse and back whence they had come.

The new baronet was either unable or unwilling to embark on a military career, which young Lawrence always found rather disappointing, especially in view of those splendid portraits in the Hall. All except his grandfather had been portrayed in colourful military uniforms, with red ribbons and plumes, stars and medals. But his grandfather had been painted in a black coat and waistcoat and, worse still, there was his shaven upper lip – just like Mr. Basham's! Lawrence decided that he must take action to restore the family honour. When he was old enough, he must join the Army. But, how could he go about it when the time came? He must seek advice, and he knew one man who would be able to tell him everything – Mr. Walker, one of the under-gardeners. He had been in the Army and, what is more, he had served his time as a 'private' soldier, which sounded to Lawrence rather select and exclusive.

Elijah Walker, a tall, erect, ginger-bearded man, was busy trenching celery when Lawrence approached him, but he was only too happy to plant his spade firmly in the soil and offer his advice. It was to prove a fateful meeting, however, by the end of which he had effectively destroyed the young Master's military aspirations.

The conversation began well enough with the choice of regiment. Elijah Walker had served his time in the Norfolks, but his considered opinion was that young Lawrence was worthy of the Lancers. By the time he had described in detail the colourful uniform worn by officers in that regiment (no thoughts of camouflage in those days!) the matter was settled. He would join the Lancers.

Having decided upon the regiment, the discussion turned to the question of promotion. To Lawrence's surprise, Elijah Walker saw no advantages in the privacy of a 'private' soldier. No – he must start as an officer, probably a lieutenant. Then, as Elijah continued his deliberations, promotions came in a steady stream. Lawrence became a Captain in no time, a Major almost in Elijah's next breath, and then a Colonel – and a fine upstanding one he would be, said his adviser. His step up to Brigadier-General took slightly longer, since the meaning of a brigade had to be explained, but, that grasped, he suddenly found himself a Major-General. There he stood, hand on hip by the Cranmer asparagus bed, already commanding a division. Then, promoted to full General, he believed himself to be within one step of his destiny and he was taken aback to learn, for the first time, of the existence of Field-Marshals. Elijah lingered lovingly over this stage of the conversation, telling the boy that Lord Wolseley was a Field-Marshal and the greatest soldier of them all.

"Then was he the Commander-in-Chief?" asked his enquirer.

Then and there the blow fell as a look of pride spread over Elijah's face and he drew himself up into an even more erect stance.

"Oh, no, Master Lawrence," he said. "Nobody can be Commander-in-Chief except His Royal Highness himself".

With that, Elijah, hitherto so sympathetic, took up his spade and calmly went on trenching celery. But in those few seconds he had destroyed Lawrence's noble ambition. All was over; a military career, so ardently looked forward to, was not for him. There was no future in it.

Not long after that sad encounter with Elijah Walker, a visitor to Cranmer asked the children, over luncheon, what they hoped to be. "A soldier," said the eldest son. "A sailor," said a younger one. Lawrence said nothing. He was pressed, but refused to answer. "Had he not made up his mind?" Yes, he had made up his mind, but he couldn't possibly tell it. His face grew red, and his mother, sensing his embarrassment, changed the subject. Later, she took him aside and beseeched him to whisper, in her secret ear, his life's objective. Eventually, he succumbed.

"The Poet Laureate," he whispered.

He knew there could only be one of them, and, more to the point, acquisition of that title was not dependent upon Royal birth.

One thing which must be said about the Jones children is that never, at any time, did they feel any sense of superiority over the lesser mortals who lived around them on the estate. They never doubted that they lived in a world of pre-ordained classes, but there the situation ended. They felt no sense of patronage when, on Christmas Eve, the cottagers on the estate crowded into the decorated Servants' Hall to receive seasonal largesse from the Squire. Each man would bring with him the traditional, extremely large, red-and-white spotted handkerchief, which would be spread upon a long trestle table. Then, with their bare hands, the children would place upon each handkerchief a large chunk of raw beef and a packet of raisins done up in thick purple paper with a sprig of holly stuck into it. This done, it was time for the Squire to come in and wish them all a Merry Christmas, and they wished him the same, not forgetting the young ladies and gentlemen.

The children were not class-conscious, because class was simply something that was there, like so many other things in their world. Moreover, the cottagers were all their respected friends, who simply happened to be 'the poor' and consequently could not expect to dine off turkey and plum pudding. Indeed, when the children visited them in their homes, they were prone to envy them the warmth and cosiness of their cottages – and the shell-boxes, the grandfather clocks and the china dogs on the mantlepiece – rather than to compare those cramped dwellings unfavourably with their own.

Nobody told them that the widow Grimmer was bringing up two boys on five shillings a week from the parish. Did the Squire, "the kindest of men", know this? He was paying his farm labourers, married men with families, fourteen shillings a week – but they were lucky, for they got free milk and butter from their Master's dairy. And did the Squire know that young Willy Woodhouse, aged seventeen, who worked in the carpenters' shop, walked seven miles in the morning, with his toolbag on his back, to repair the barn at Kettlestone, and seven miles home again at night? Old John Button, the head carpenter, drove there in his cart to keep an eye on the work. The Squire held John Button in very high regard, but surely he could not have known that, if his head carpenter was about to return from Kettlestone half an hour before knocking-off time, not once did it occur to him to wait and give his workmen a lift home in his pony cart. He rode, as befitted his status, and Sam and young Willy trudged again the seven miles of dusty lanes. Estate carpenters in those days, like the children of the Squire, received class as something 'given', together with most of the men of the place. Hard work, thoroughness, and pride in the job were the marks of those men; their patience, endurance and self-discipline were taken for granted by themselves as much as by their employer.

But, as the nineteenth century ran through its final years, great changes were taking place – and not for the better. Agriculture was in a state of great depression. There was much talk in the Hall of agricultural wages, of low rents and rents remitted. Economies had to be made and, one by one, the laundry was closed, the footman left and, after him, the groom; Mr. Basham retired from the garden and was not replaced; and the Squire's riding horse was sold.

But much worse was to follow in the next few years, and by no means all of it could be blamed on the parlous state of agriculture. From being a representative family of the Norfolk squirearchy managing to get along with a butler, housekeeper, cook and kitchen maid, three housemaids, two laundry maids, two nurses, a coachman, four gardeners, two gamekeepers, two woodmen and two estate carpenters, they were to become a family of exiles, wandering about the Continent, rootless and, in the eyes of their Norfolk neighbours, decidedly peculiar. And it was all brought about by Great-Aunt Rachel's Will.

It transpired that, although he had inherited the baronetcy and the Squiredom, Lawrence's father did not own Cranmer Hall. It had passed, by the age-old tradition of primogeniture, to his uncle (Lawrence's great-uncle) who was the local parson, holding the family living for thirty years. He had married Rachel Gurney, a woman of strong character, an antiquarian and genealogist with the added talent of being able to paint birds and butterflies. Lawrence's great-uncle trusted her in all matters and, on his death, left all his possessions to her absolutely, confident in the belief that she, being childless, would pass the Hall back to her eldest nephew. Unfortunately, his assumption was not translated into reality, and it was a Gurney relation of hers who acquired the benefit and immediately decreed that Cranmer Hall and the Estate must be let.

Unfortunately, Lawrence's father was in no position to meet the cost of tenancy, and thus the family left these shores to start a new life on the Continent, where living costs were considered to be more within their means. The children were undoubtedly fortunate in having parents who, at such a time of crisis, possessed the ability to take stock of the situation, work out a plan and start all over again.

The years that lay ahead were to provide a fascinating story, though a totally different one from that of the apparently affluent Norfolk family living at 'The Hall'. As far as Lawrence was concerned, however, much of his future followed the pattern which had been pre-ordained for him, for his name had been 'put down' for Eton immediately on his birth. The fact that he was able to take his place there, in the hallowed tradition of the family, was due to a legacy from a soldier uncle, who died prematurely in Burma from not changing his wet clothes after snipe-shooting. Then it was on to Oxford, from where he emerged to take up a career in investment banking – far removed, perhaps, from his boyhood ambitions of soldiering and becoming Poet laureate, but it could be said that, at different times, he briefly flirted with both. Twenty years after his discussions with Elijah Walker near the Cranmer asparagus bed, he was wounded in battle in the French countryside – but he was a mere lieutenant, the battle had been lost and the British Army was in headlong retreat. As regards his literary aspirations, though he may not have challenged the Poet Laureate, he produced a number of books of prose in a style which drew high praise in literary circles, with the "Punch" critic declaring that "Sir Lawrence is one of the Joneses who should certainly be kept up with".

It is clear that, throughout his life, Lawrence Jones made use of the privileges which that silver spoon offered, whilst, at the same time, overcoming the handicaps which it also brought with it.

As for me, however – I think I'll settle for E.P.N.S.

>─┤─◄►─O─◄►─┤─◄

Parson Woodforde Meets Hannah Snell.

June 21st, 1778: I walked up to the White Hart (at Weston Longville) with Mr. Lewis and Bill to see a famous Woman in Men's Cloaths, by name Hannah Snell, who was 21 years as a common soldier in the Army, and not discovered by any as a woman. Cousin Lewis had mounted guard with her abroad. She went in the Army by the name of John Gray. She has a Pension from the Crown now of £18.5.0. per annum and the liberty of wearing Men's Cloaths and also a Cockade in her Hat, which she still wears. She has laid in a room with 70 soldiers and not discovered by any of them. The forefinger of her right hand was cut off by a Sword at the taking of Pondicherry. She is now about 60 yrs of age and talks very sensible and well, and travels the country with a Basket at her back, selling Buttons, Garters, laces, &c. I took 4 Pr of 4d Buttons and gave her 0.2.6.

The Rev. James Woodforde,
The Diary of a Country Parson.

I Went To Cley.

It was dull in May
When I went astray
And visited friends down Devonshire way.
I didn't care
For so far from Yare
And only politeness held me there!

    But I went to Cley
    In early July
    When wild rose blushed and the tides were high.
    The blackbird piped
    In the inland dells
    By Walsingham, Warham and Wighton and Wells.

It rained in June
When I went to Troon
(They said it had something to do with the moon).
The chilly scene
Was all grey and green
My only comfort to say I'd been!

    So I went to Cley
    In early July
    When cattle by Glaven 'mid meadowsweet lie
    And scent of elder
    Is weaving spells
    Round Sheringham, Salthouse and Stiffkey and Wells.

I'll always remember
North Wales in September
With sepia peaks in cloud-topped splendour.
I looked with awe
Upon all I saw
And my heart fled back to a marsh-fringed shore!

     So give me Cley
     In early July
     When mallow in Morston is banked waist-high.
     And oh! for the tale
     The wild tern tells
     By Brancaster, Burnham and Blakeney and Wells!

Joan Watson-Cook

July.

A Village on the Cliff.

It is morning at Cromer, the sun high in the heavens, a strong north-west wind blowing, the sea just flecked with white, and a good prospect of fair weather at last. The air, coming in fresh to the bedroom window, has already new life in it; no sound is heard above the wind but the fisherman calling lobsters in the streets. Although so early on this bright summer morning, already there is one sight that is missed. From the very window with the sea outlook it might be possible, had not sleep been so strong, to behold a sunrise as beautiful as any to drag visitors out of their beds. For Cromer, let me tell you, is one of the few watering-places where, in the summer months, you can, from the same window, see the sun rise straight out of the ocean at morning, and the sun disappear in the glory of orange and scarlet in the evening.

As yet, however, I have noticed no disposition to study sunrises at Cromer. The air is so laden with sleep, the whole district is so covered with poppies, that the four o'clock arousing is, I find, indefinitely postponed. Young ladies leaning upon the Cromer balconies after breakfast make up their minds to see the sun rise the very next morning, but somehow or other their good resolutions fail them, and so far we have had to depend for description of them on the Cromer fishermen and boatmen, who highly extol the beauties we have lost, with a view, no doubt, to an arrangement whereby a better view of the sunrise might be obtained from the deck of the *Maud* or the *Alice*.

So let us mount to the cliffs up there by the white lighthouse, which is so prominent a feature in the landscape. This is, perhaps, the best spot in all Cromer. They say that the Cromer cliffs are gradually falling away, that the sea has registered a vow to make an end of this charming little village; landslips after landslips have given their customary warning, and scarce a winter passes without some arable acres falling into the hungry ocean. Indeed the inhabitants, to preserve their houses over their heads, have been compelled to fortify the village with strong sea walls, fearing lest red-roofed street, grey church and all, should one day topple over

Cromer. From East Cliff.

The cliffs of Cromer.

into the sand, and Cromer be a matter of history. It is for this purpose that the latest lighthouse has been erected, far back on the Cromer grass cliffs, lest it should fall, as did its immediate predecessors, into the sea.

Once mounted to the Lighthouse Point, Cromer may be viewed at its very best. The cliffs for miles round are covered with an undergrowth of fern and heather, divided by green paths as firm and true as a billiard table. No glaring white is to be seen anywhere; the cliffs are brown and sandy, the sea blue, the landscape of a universal green. Once up here you can wander for miles along the cliff in peace and quiet, amongst farms and cornfields, and such a variety of wild flowers as I have rarely seen collected together. The brilliant scarlet of the poppy, growing not only in the cornfield, but in masses and borderings at the cliff's edge; the bright gold of the wild yellow tulip, an inhabitant of these favourite districts; the deep mauve of the Scotch thistle, and the constant purple of the heather make Cromer cliffs a veritable flower garden – a rare accessory to any English seaside place.

On these cliffs, never deserted by a breeze, surrounded by scenery so rich and varied with farm land and wood on one hand and the uncomplaining sea on the other, it would be strange indeed if a luxurious morning could not well be spent, a morning of that idleness which is no stranger to reflection or imagination. Here, resting on the cliff amongst the wild flowers, the blue sky overhead, the air exhilarating, the martins and swallows darting from their holes in pursuit of insects, the corn waving as the breezes sweep across the fields, the sea face chequered with purple and blue as the clouds flit over the surface, away from the madding crowd, from noise and din and discord and vulgarity, seems the place where busy brains and tired frames might rest for a while and be at peace.

Clement Scott.
(From *A Village on the Cliff*, 1886).

The Secret Garden.

There was a time, many years ago, when I firmly believed that I knew every little corner of Norwich. It was no idle boast for I had spent countless hours exploring the city which had captured my boyhood heart from the very day when I first set eyes upon it.

It was in 1932 that the demands of my father's profession caused the family to take up residence in the city and, from then until the outbreak of the Second World War, I devoted much of my time to finding out more about the love of my life. Large and small, attractive and ugly – every facet from Castle to courtyard and from pristine street to down-trodden alley came within my compass. Of course, exploring the city was a much more straightforward business in those days, for there was not the continuous competition with ever-increasing motor traffic which now exists, and my exploration called for nothing more than a bicycle and a willing pair of legs. Even the trams, threatening though they were, presented only the slightest of obstacles, for manoeuvrability was more important than sheer bulk, and those iron monsters were no match for a boy on a bike!

By the time the Second World War came upon us, my familiarity with Norwich seemed complete and, though there were blemishes here and there, I was very fond of "my" city. Then, like so many others, I went away, and it was to be the late 1940s before I returned. By that time, of course, there had been changes. There had been some "knocking down" and some "putting up", but that was only to be expected, and they were the sort of changes which would only be noticeable to somebody coming upon them for the first time. Yet it was not merely changes that I noticed for, indulging in my perambulations on foot, which was my preferred means of travel, I suddenly found myself coming upon parts of the city whose presence had previously escaped me, though they had been there all the time. Perhaps I was now seeing my city, for the first time, through the eyes of an adult, and there was one such discovery which was to have a lasting effect on me.

I had made my way down through the hustle and bustle of Prince of Wales Road and turned into St. Faith's Lane on my way to keep an appointment at the nearby Horsefair House when, on the corner of Recorder Road, I came upon an attractive pair of wrought-iron gates. I had passed these gates many times previously, and I had even read the inscription which proclaimed it to be the "James Stuart Garden", but I knew nothing of the identity of James Stuart and, furthermore, the gates had always been closed. On this occasion, however, one of them stood invitingly open and, aware that I was early for my appointment, I decided to venture inside.

I found myself under an arch which gave no indication of what lay within, and I felt rather like one of the children in Frances Hodgson Burnett's *Secret Garden,* for that was what it was. There before me were neatly-tended flower beds and rose borders, within which lay a close-cropped lawn which was not just a lawn, but a bowling green, used by a local club. And, strategically placed around the perimeter, there were rustic wooden seats where visitors could sit and enjoy the tranquillity such a short distance from the tumultuous hurly-burly of the city streets. I accepted the invitation and sat for a while, thanking those of our forefathers who realised that small green oases such as that garden achieve just as much in making Norwich a fine city as do any amount of fine buildings.

What man, I thought, could ask for a better memorial than that haven of peace? Who, indeed, was James Stuart?

When James Stuart died, on October 12th, 1913, he was described as "an eminent Victorian", "divinely favoured" and, more pointedly, "a man whose achievements are worthy to be remembered by the citizens of Norwich". In truth, however, he was not a native son of the city for, like many another man of greatness, he had come from away, made Norwich his home and, by virtue of his sincerity, won the hearts of its citizens, who were happy to adopt him as one of them.

He was, in fact, a Scot, having been born in the village of Balgonie, in Fife, on January 2nd, 1843. The son of a prosperous mill owner, he quite naturally grew up amongst machinery and working people, two factors which were to greatly affect his future life. He was destined to become an academic, though his interests and his influence were to cover a much wider field. He began with a brilliant career at St. Andrew's University and then travelled south to achieve even greater distinction at Cambridge, becoming

Master of Arts and Doctor of Laws and then, in 1867, being elected a Fellow of Trinity. It was then that, still at the tender age of 24, he was appointed the University's first Professor of Applied Mechanics, a position which he held for fourteen years.

Throughout those academic years, however, he retained clear memories of the deprivation he had seen amongst "the lower classes of society". There had been an occasion when he had spent a week with a hospitable Northumbrian miner and his family in their little pit cottage. There were just two bedrooms, one being occupied by the miner and his wife whilst he, himself, shared the other with their three stalwart sons, who all worked in the pits. At different hours during the night, according to their shifts at work, the men would rise from their beds and set off. Then, at the end of the day, they and their neighbours all washed at a communal tap in the backyard.

He deplored, also, the lack of educational facilities, particularly amongst the womenfolk, deprived, as they were, of "even just a few rays of the light, which ought to be as brilliant as coming from a university, even in the cities and towns which do not have the opportunities which universities afford".

To this end, he proposed the formation of a kind of peripatetic university, the idea being that lecturers would tour over a wide area bringing some of the benefits of university education to those who, because of social class, gender or any other reason, would otherwise be cut off from it. It became known as the University Extension Movement and was an immediate success, so much so that, within a few short weeks, he was travelling north from Cambridge, in response to a request from a committee of ladies in Yorkshire, to give scientific lectures in that area of the country.

Almost immediately, there followed another trip to the North of England which was to give him, in the nicest possible way, the shock of his life. It was in Crewe, where he was to address a group of working men in the local Mechanics' Institute on the subject of Meteors, and he anticipated an audience of perhaps a score or so. Imagine his amazement, therefore, to find the hall packed with 1500 people. It was not, however, his personal magnetism that had attracted them, but rather the fact that on the previous evening, by a fantastic stroke of fortune, the skies above Crewe had provided their own firework display in the shape of a spectacular meteoric shower. One can only think it was this incident which later led to his being described as "divinely favoured".

There is no doubt that Education was James Stuart's first love, perhaps his chief love, all through his life, but it was by no means the be-all and end-all of his existence. Indeed, the reverse was the case, for he was a versatile man and in his time played many parts and responded to many enthusiasms. Those who knew him best said that his most striking characteristics were his versatility and his grasp of detail. Whatever the subject he took up he learnt thoroughly, which made him a tough customer to argue with, especially as he took up more subjects than most men.

In view of all this, it is not surprising that he should have become a Member of Parliament, though he failed miserably at the first attempt. That was in 1882, when he stood for the University constituency at Cambridge, but he was a Liberal while the University was a hotbed of Conservatism, so his defeat was not unexpected. Two years later, however, he entered the House of Commons after winning a by-election for the Town constituency. Then followed a period as Member for Hackney, after which he transferred to the Hoxton Division of Shoreditch, a seat which he held for fifteen years.

Meanwhile, James Stuart found his way into journalism when the Liberal Party wanted an outlet for its views. The starting of a newspaper, especially in London, was not a venture to be undertaken with a light heart, for the pavements of Fleet Street were strewn with the wreckage of countless such enterprises. He it was, however, who founded – and for a time edited – *The Star,* later to be followed by the *Morning Leader,* which eventually merged with the *Daily News.*

Meanwhile, the University Extension Movement received his full attention as its influence spread throughout the country, and it was this brainchild of his that was to bring him to Norwich. The Movement had become firmly established in the city, where one of its most prominent figures was Laura Elizabeth Colman, daughter of Jeremiah James Colman, founder of the firm which made the word 'mustard' synonymous with the name of the city in which he produced it. Inevitably they met, and gradually romance blossomed. Then, on July 16th, 1890, they married.

The wedding, at Prince's Street Congregational Church, was a splendid occasion. "Rarely, if ever," said the *Eastern Daily Press,* "has a domestic event awakened such a widespread and kindly interest among the residents of Norwich, and indeed far beyond. Naturally," it went on, in the colourful, high-flown phraseology so beloved by writers of that time, "everyone desired that the heavens should smile upon the wedding day of a pair who have shown practical sympathy with various movements beneficial to the community. The thousands of friends and well-wishers of the bride and bridegroom were accordingly rejoiced to find that the morning of the wedding day opened with an auspicious brightness which had as perfect a realisation as could be desired".

The members of the bridal party were conveyed to the church in eleven carriages, along gaily decorated streets, and waved on their way by admiring onlookers. The wedding breakfast was served in Carrow Priory, in the upper room of which "the numerous and valuable wedding presents were arrayed". For the benefit of those people not privileged to be present, the *Eastern Daily Press,* in accordance with the custom of the day, published a comprehensive list.

The employees of the family firm presented the bride with a diamond bracelet, accompanied by a letter which, I feel, clearly indicates the degree of mutual affection which existed between employers and staff:

Carrow Works, Norwich, June 28th, 1890.

DEAR MISS COLMAN – I am deputed by the travellers, clerks, and workpeople in the employ of your father's firm at Carrow Works to ask your acceptance of the accompanying diamond bracelet on the occasion of your marriage.

Many of them, from a long and happy connection with the firm, have come to feel a very warm interest in everything which concerns the well-being of the family at Carrow House, and they have, therefore, a natural desire to mark this auspicious occasion as a joyful family event; but they also feel under obligation to testify their appreciation of your earnest personal sympathy with the many things which have been done to advance their best interests, both moral and material; and they avail themselves of this fitting opportunity to beg that you will accept this gift as being at once a recognition of your good feeling towards them, and an expression of their most cordial wishes for the happiness of yourself and your husband in the new relations of life upon which you are about to enter.

With every sentiment of regard, I am, dear Miss Colman, yours sincerely, (Signed) Robt. Haselwood.

James Stuart, M.A., LL.D. Privy Councillor.

Laura Elizabeth Stuart, O.B.E. Member of Norwich City Council and the first woman J.P. appointed for the City.

All work at Carrow had ceased at noon on the day of the wedding, and every employee was presented with a souvenir of the happy event, though the nature of those souvenirs does not appear to be recorded. It is known, however, that arrangements were made with the railway company on the workers' behalf to take them to the seaside "at excursion rates".

Eventually, amid a shower of rice, the bride and groom emerged from Carrow and travelled to Trowse Station to catch the five o'clock train and set off on their honeymoon.

On their return, James and Laura Stuart made their home at Carrow Abbey, suitably altered and refurbished for the purpose. It was to be much more than just a home, however, and, over the next twenty or so years, there were to be few people of eminence in the worlds of literature, art, science, politics, or any other form of human endeavour who were not entertained there at some time or other. Members of Royalty also found their way within its portals, and it was there that the Prince and Princess of Wales (later King Edward VII and Queen Alexandra) took lunch when they drove to Norwich in 1900 to open the new Jenny Lind Hospital for Sick Children.

James Stuart took it all in his stride, for he had walked with men of greatness, from Charles Darwin to William Booth and from Robert Browning to Alfred Lord Tennyson. Through his Liberal beliefs, he had also become the friend and close associate of Gladstone. Yet it was by no means a one-man success story, for he and his wife made an ideal partnership, continuously working together in support of every cause that came within their compass. Throughout her life the former Laura Colman, together with her sisters, Ethel and Helen, felt great concern for the well-being of the poorer members of Norwich society. The city slums and the degree of deprivation within them were a constant source of worry, and the new partnership worked together to improve conditions for the lower classes.

It was not that James Stuart became the figurehead in local organisations, for, though he was for a number of years Chairman of the Governors of Norwich Grammar School and President of the local Liberal Association, his best work was always carried out in the background. He developed the habit, whenever time permitted, of turning up unexpectedly at some meeting or other and offering help. "He was," they said, "always there when he was needed".

It was following the death of Jeremiah Colman in 1898 that Dr. Stuart became a director of J. & J. Colman, Ltd. and even his great capacity for work was strained by the demands made on him at Carrow. Nevertheless, he applied himself to this new task and rapidly exploded the long-established myth that an academic can never become a successful man of business. Lord Cozens-Hardy, who knew him as well as anybody, declared that "nobody connected with Carrow would ever hesitate to say that he was as good and astute a man of business as ever had anything to do with the affairs of that great company".

Much of his work was dedicated to improving the lot of the Company's workers, and he was the main instigator of the private pension scheme to see them through their later years. Every facet of their lives was considered, from instructional courses in all manner of subjects and the provision of recreational facilities to caring for them in times of sickness or domestic hardship. In my own boyhood, it was widely acknowledged that the most contented workers in the entire city of Norwich were those employed at Colman's.

James Stuart happily adopted Norwich as his home city and developed a deep love for the place and its people, yet he never lost the traces of his origin. "He never could have been mistaken for a Norfolk man," said Lord Cozens-Hardy. "He was proud, and justly proud, of his origin". But the people of Norwich loved him just as much for all that, for he was a man of great tenderness, deeply sympathetic and the possessor of one of God's greatest gifts – a genius for making friends.

There was an occasion when he and Mrs. Stuart were entertaining the inmates of the Blind Asylum in the garden at the Abbey. He invited a friend to accompany him to meet some of his guests and, on the way, he popped into his study to collect some cigars to distribute among his visitors. He had a varied stock, from which he selected a brand which he thought suitable for the occasion. Then he suddenly put the box back and chose instead one containing some of the finest cigars that he had in his possession, remarking to his friend as he did so, "If you make a gift, give your best".

His tenderness, furthermore, was not confined to his fellow human beings, for he was a great lover of animals, especially dogs. The story has long been told of the occasion when he carried in his arms for fully a mile a favourite dog which had accidentally met with an injury and could not get home without help.

Hence it seems all the more unjust that such a man should suddenly, in 1909, be struck down so unexpectedly with the devastating illness which was to leave him with that lively, alert mind encapsulated within a feeble and unresponding body. The people of Norwich were stunned into silence and prayed that their adopted son might somehow be restored to fitness, but it was not to be. For four long years, with never a suggestion of complaint, he suffered the agonising frustration of his condition, mentally alert yet physically incapable of action. Then, just before midnight on Sunday October 12th, 1913, death brought its relief.

On the following Wednesday a private service was held at Carrow Abbey, after which the coffin, draped with the robes that he had worn as Lord Rector of St. Andrew's University, was taken for interment in the Colman family plot at the Rosary. Black shutters and flags at half-mast were seen throughout the city, and the Rosary paths and the entire route from Carrow were full of sombre-faced mourners. Norwich had lost a dear friend.

Not unexpectedly, a wealth of glowing tributes was immediately forthcoming, not only in Norwich but also in the many other parts of Britain where James Stuart's presence had been felt. There was much talk of memorials – a wall tablet or even, perhaps, a statue – but the most touching and, at the same time, the most worthwhile came from his two sisters-in-law, the Misses Ethel and Helen Colman. In common with their sister, they had long wished to do something to ease the plight of those people in the city living in sub-standard conditions, and this was their opportunity to act. They would build some houses, "half-way, as it were, between ordinary small working-class houses and endowed almshouses such as are provided by some of the charitable trusts".

Thus is was that, on the newly-developed Recorder Road, there came into being a block of 22 houses, to be let at a low rent. Each one was self-contained – and each had a bath! They were tastefully designed, with a touch of Dutch influence in their style, by Edward Boardman & Son, and they remain to this day a delight to behold. They were to be run on a charitable basis and, as a mark of the strong and abiding affection that existed between the two ladies and their beloved brother-in-law, they would be called "Stuart Court".

It was on Tuesday, September 18th, 1915 that, in the presence of a distinguished invited company, Stuart Court was officially

Opening the James Stuart Garden – The Town Clerk (Mr. Arnold Miller), the Misses Ethel and Helen Colman, the Lord Mayor (Sir Henry Holmes), Mr. Russell Colman, the Lord Bishop of Norwich, the Sheriff (Mr. Harper-Smith) and his wife, and Mr. Sydney Cozens-Hardy.

The Opening Ceremony.

opened by the Master of the Rolls, Lord Cozens-Hardy, who happened also to be the uncle of the ladies who had brought the splendid development to fruition.

Meanwhile, their sister also had plans for a memorial to her late husband, and her eyes fell upon a piece of land on the opposite side of Recorder Road, at its junction with St. Faith's Lane. She acquired it and began to apply her mind to the form which her memorial would take. Not for her would there be bricks and mortar; her vision was of a quiet garden where people like me could escape for a while from the pressures of life and breathe the peaceful air of Nature.

Sadly, because of delays brought about by the conditions of War, she did not live to see the realisation of her dream. Her worthy sisters, however, welcomed the return of Peace by creating the kind of haven she had envisaged. Then, on Wednesday, July 19th, 1922, they led the Lord Mayor and a band of other city worthies to formally open the wrought-iron gates of the "James Stuart Garden".

It was a little lung to help the city breathe – just as important, in my view, as the houses they themselves had brought into being, for, if I may ever-so-slightly paraphrase the words of W.H. Davies,

> *What is this life if, full of care,*
> *We have no time to sit and stare?*

Sir Peter Eade – City Father.

It was in 1848 that the newly-qualified Dr. Peter Eade dragged himself away from London and went back to Blofield to assist his father in his practice. It was to be a merely temporary expedient, and he promised himself that, as soon as he had amassed sufficient funds, there would be a speedy return to the lifestyle which had so greatly pleased him in the previous few years. As everybody knows, however, it takes circumstances of great magnitude to make a true son of Norfolk sever his roots and leave his native county, and so it proved with the young doctor. It was not long before he realised that country living, especially with the chance to engage in his favourite pastime of horseriding, was what he really wanted.

Then, in 1856, he was elected an Honorary Physician to the Norwich Public Dispensary, an organisation which catered purely for out-patients, many of whom he visited in their own homes. This was his first step on the local medical ladder, and he soon decided to settle in Norwich and pursue his medical career in that city. He then encountered something which many doctors (and, indeed, dentists) have always experienced – the penalty of looking youthful. I suppose, in today's parlance, one might call it 'reverse ageism', for there are many people who would shun the services of a newly-arrived practitioner, however highly-qualified he might be, in favour of those of an older man.

"Being then not thirty years of age and very young looking", he wrote, "almost necessarily consulting practice came slowly. But even at first I received some fees, and during the first year these amounted to nearly one hundred guineas".

A year or so later, Dr. Goodwin, one of the Physicians to the Norfolk and Norwich Hospital, relinquished the appointment, and Dr. Eade was chosen to take his place. Having previously lived in lodgings on Bank Plain, he now moved to Dr. Goodwin's house in Queen Street, and thus began his direct association with the Hospital which was to continue for 53 years until, in 1911, he became one of its first Vice-Presidents.

Before long, busy though he was with both private and hospital practice, he began to miss the outdoor exercise to which he had been accustomed in the country. As luck would have it, a Mounted Volunteer Corps known as the 'Norfolk Light Horse' had recently been formed under the command of Captain F. Hay Gurney and, being an experienced horseman, Peter Eade became one of their number. They were mostly the sons of gentlemen and, though they welcomed the chance to ride, it cannot be denied that their uniform also was by no means an unimportant feature of their soldiering. It was a rather splendid outfit, consisting, as described in the *Norfolk Chronicle* in March, 1861, of "scarlet tunic with blue facings, white cross belt, white breeches and Napoleon boots. The head-dress was a busby with blue bag; the forage cap was blue trimmed with white". The young doctor recorded his pride at wearing it, especially on ceremonial occasions, but also admitted the difficulty they had in keeping their head-dress upon their heads during a smart gallop, "even though various devices were tried for securing fixity of tenure".

A few years after taking up residence in Queen Street, Peter Eade, steadily climbing the ladder of success, was destined to move once more. Yet again the move was prompted by the retirement of a colleague, it being on this occasion Dr. Ranking, one of the City's foremost physicians, whose failing health compelled him to give up practice and vacate the splendid house which he occupied in Upper St. Giles' Street. The house was owned by the Rev. John Methwold, Vicar of Wighton, and Peter Eade quickly stepped in to take over the tenancy. It was an extremely vast property for occupation by a lone, 40-year-old bachelor, and his professional earnings at that time hardly justified such a bold step. The result of the venture, however, was highly satisfactory, for his practice immediately began to increase with great rapidity. In any case, the occupancy of the many-roomed mansion was set to double some five years later when he married Ellen, the only daughter of Hugh Rump, of Wells-next-the-Sea. Sadly, the building was not destined to echo to the patter of children's feet – not, that is, until some years later, when it became the Norwich High School for Boys, where the actor, Sir John Mills, received his early education.

In the years that followed, Dr. Eade was to become one of the most highly-respected and best-loved medical men of his time, not only by his patients but also by his professional colleagues. His private practice grew extensively, but he was also proud of 'his'

Sir Peter Eade's house in Upper St. Giles, Norwich.

hospital and never lost the opportunity to acquire adjacent pieces of land and to raise the money needed to extend its buildings. "The very name of the Hospital has always been a talisman for opening purse strings," he said.

He was a great upholder of moral values and, on January 4th, 1871, the centenary of the Hospital's foundation, an extremely lengthy letter from him was published in the *Norwich Mercury*. To him, the Hospital was not just a place for curing physical ills, for many of the poorer patients were in need of other help. These were his words:

> *Let it always be remembered that, in addition to its other means of usefulness, a residence in the Hospital for a few weeks is in itself a most powerful means of teaching the neglected and ignorant such things as order, management, hygiene, manners and, let us hope, morals, which may bear the most valuable fruit in after life. The daily contemplation, as a matter of course, of clean beds; of wards so neat and fresh as ours, and so tastefully restored and decorated, as they have been through the liberality of recent benefactors; of a well-kept and handsomely-planted garden; and the being accustomed to the daily discipline of the establishment – all these things cannot fail to educate the mind and to elevate the tone of the patient, so that he leaves the Hospital a better member of society than when he entered it.*

On November 20th, 1876, a meeting was held in St. Andrew's Hall for the purpose of raising the sum of £35,000 for the enlargement and improvement of the Norfolk and Norwich Hospital. The Earl of Leicester, President of the Hospital, was in the Chair, and the Prince and Princess of Wales travelled from Sandringham to attend. It was a very large meeting, and probably the most influential that had ever been held in Norwich. A very large sum of money was promised at the meeting, including £5,000 from the Earl of Leicester, who also promised a further sum of £13,000 as soon as the remainder had been raised.

Shortly afterwards, it was decided not to enlarge the old hospital, but to build a new one, and a Building Committee was formed. Needless to say, Peter Eade was a member of that committee.

It is, I believe, worthy of mention that he was also Physician to the Jenny Lind Infirmary for Sick Children and the Great Hospital in Bishopgate, as well as Medical Visitor to the Catton Grove Asylum – and, somehow or other, he also found time to carry out the duties of a City magistrate, as well as being Honorary Manager of the Norfolk and Norwich Trustee Savings Bank.

Even this, however, was by no means the end of this remarkable man's commitments. "Almost from the first," he wrote, "I had felt a desire to engage in some of the general work of the City as a relief from my professional work". Hence, in 1876, he became a Director of the Norwich Union Life Insurance Society, an appointment to which he gave his full and thorough attention until his death nearly 40 years later.

It is, I believe, patently clear that the two great commitments of Peter Eade's life – medical and financial – would have sorely tested a lesser man. For him, however, the reverse was the case, and there came a time when his hectic public life developed a third facet. It was, indeed, this third aspect of his life which made his reputation as one of the greatest of all citizens of Norwich, and his life story from that time onward is, in itself, almost a complete history of the City of that period.

It all began in the autumn of 1869 when he was persuaded to become a candidate for election to the Norwich Town Council, as it was then known. He was duly elected and went on to serve his City for many years, becoming Sheriff in 1880 and three times its Mayor. His highest accolade, however, came in 1885, when the honour of knighthood was bestowed upon him by Queen Victoria.

Throughout the years of his civic life two objectives were always uppermost in his mind – the protection and enhancement of the City of Norwich, and the improvement in the quality of life of its citizens. The need for the latter was regularly brought home to him, both in the course of his hospital work and, even more, when he visited patients in their homes. It was a time of great poverty and deprivation among the lower classes, especially those who, born in the 500 courts and yards of Norwich, never had any certainty of either health or employment.

One way in which he felt he could achieve both his aims was by securing open spaces and public parks in various districts of the steadily growing city. In February, 1876, the *Norwich Mercury* published a letter from him calling attention to this need, and John Gurney of Sprowston Hall immediately offered the sum of £1,000 towards any scheme which included the laying out of Mousehold

Heath as a public ground. Later on, in the Town Council, he called for, and obtained, a Committee "to endeavour to promote this most desirable object".

This Committee at once commenced operations, but met with so much objection from owners, and was so thwarted by the extravagant prices asked for land, that progress was slow. Once started, however, the movement gradually and firmly took root in the public mind, to such effect that, by 1880, Peter Eade was able to report that the City then had, as public parks, 150 acres of Mousehold Heath, eighty acres of Eaton Park, and seven or eight smaller parks or recreation grounds, together with many lesser open spots. The acquisition of Mousehold Heath, however, was delayed when the previous title-holders, the Dean and Chapter of Norwich, agreed to transfer the title to the Corporation. The residents of Pockthorpe immediately claimed it as their property, and the dispute had to be settled in the Chancery Court. It was on May 12th, 1886 that the then Mayor, none other than John Gurney, opened the new road across it and dedicated the Heath to the free use of the people for ever.

One area of land which Peter Eade considered would make a splendid public recreation ground was that situated near St. Augustine's Gates and belonging to the Wingfield Charity. In view of their charitable status, however, the Trustees decided against selling the land, but they offered a long lease of it for a rental of about £400 a year. This offer was submitted to the Town Council but was turned down on account of the cost.

"The grounds would have made an admirable recreation ground," wrote Peter Eade, "and this spot commands a grand view of the river above Norwich. Indeed, the Wingfield Hill commanded a view almost to be compared to that of the Wye as seen from the town of Ross in Herefordshire".

Sadly, in a very short space of time the ground was covered with houses and forever lost to the City.

Having provided the City with public parks, Dr. Eade was eager to use these open spaces for the benefit of the citizens and, on the occasion of the Queen's birthday on May 24th, 1881, he provided a band to play in Chapel Field in her honour. The crowd of people who came to hear the band was so vast that he subsequently engaged the Carrow Works Band to play in the Gardens on every Thursday during the summer months. This was the initiation of what was to become the general custom of having a band provided by the City to play in the Field once or twice every week during the summer. I have a feeling that the audience for such a concert nowadays would be somewhat modest compared with the thousands who attended in the 1880s, but at that time it was a double attraction. For most of them it was just about their only chance to listen to 'live' music, and for many it was a great opportunity to get away, for an hour or two, from the hovels in which they lived and worked.

Some time later, music of another kind was provided by a series of organ recitals in St. Andrew's Hall. These events were held on Saturday evenings during the winter months, with the organ pieces being interspersed with various vocal items. The charge for admission was twopence, and the Hall was invariably packed to its maximum capacity. "There is no doubt," he wrote, "that this Saturday evening musical entertainment is a valuable means of agreeable recreation to those of very limited resources".

November 9th, 1880 saw the start of Peter Eade's year of office as Sheriff of Norwich. It was to be a very busy year for him, for the duties of Shrievalty are many and oncrous, and he was a great upholder of both the responsibilities and the privileges of that office.

By this time he was approaching the peak of his political career, but there were still greater pinnacles of success which lay ahead of him. The first came on November 9th, 1883, when he was elected Mayor of Norwich. It was quite a hectic day for the new First Citizen for, having entertained a large party of civic worthies to lunch at the Royal Hotel (then located, incidentally, by the Market Place), he and Mrs. Eade set off for Sandringham, where they joined some five hundred other guests at a Ball in celebration of the Prince of Wales' birthday.

A few days later he had a meeting with that other great Norwich benefactor, John Gurney, who had some disquieting news to impart concerning the future of Norwich Castle. The Castle was at that time, of course, still in use as a prison and, though the City owned much of the Castle mound and ditches, the main building was the property of the Government by way of the Prison Commissioners. For some time there had been dissatisfaction with the prison accommodation, especially as regards the female prisoners, and the Commissioners advocated complete reconstruction of the prison, which might well interfere with the architectural aspect of the Castle.

Peter Eade conveyed this news to the Council, who heard the tidings with great dismay. The suggestion was made that the City should buy the Castle from the Government, who could then spend the money on a new prison elsewhere. The trouble with that view, however, was the stipulation of the Prisons Act that, when a prison is given up, it must be sold at the price of £120 per cell, which, in this case, would amount to £10,320 – much too high a sum to put upon the County Rate. The Council decided to do what all good councils do in such situations – they appointed a sub-committee, under the Chairmanship of the Mayor. They could have done nothing better!

On February 19th, 1884, Peter Eade led a deputation to London to discuss the subject with the Home Secretary (Sir W. Vernon Harcourt). On June 17th he was able to announce to the Corporation that the Government had agreed to sell to the City 'the Castle and its Environments' for £4,000. Not surprisingly, the Town Council agreed to the purchase and, as a result, a new prison was erected on the border of Mousehold Heath.

It is worth noting that the Prison Commissioners, in a separate deal, also took over the old City Gaol. Although the statutory price for this building was £5,425, the price received by the City was, in fact, £7,505, which made the purchase of the Castle an even greater bargain!

Almost the last important act of Peter Eade's Mayoralty was to sign the contract with the Government for the purchase of the Castle, and eventually, on August 2nd, 1887, the County and City prisoners were transferred to Mousehold. Finally, on September 12th of that year, formal possession of the Castle was given to the Corporation.

Long before the negotiations had been finally concluded, a marked change had come over the principal player, for Doctor Peter Eade had become Sir Peter. On June 3rd, 1885 he had received a letter from the Prime Minister (Mr. Gladstone) telling him that Queen Victoria proposed to honour him with a knighthood, and on August 1st he presented himself at Osborne House on the Isle of Wight to receive the honour from her hands.

It was not until October 23rd, 1894 that the Castle was re-opened in its new guise, and it seems fitting that, at that time, he was serving his second term as Mayor. I feel I can do no better than to let Sir Peter recount in his own words the happenings of that day when the Duke and Duchess of York came to carry out the formal opening ceremony:

The Castle has now been entirely re-modelled internally, and its prison wards have been converted into a series of rooms adapted to the purpose of a museum. The whole building has been fitted with electric light, and is warmed throughout by hot air.

The Duke and Duchess of York were received at Thorpe Station by me (Mayor), the Sheriff of Norwich, the High Sheriff and others. They drove thence, escorted by some of the 1st King's Dragoon Guards, to the Castle, where they were presented with an Address by the Corporation. After having made a tour of the buildings, the Royal party and a few other guests were entertained at luncheon by me, the Mayor, in the Picture Gallery. The great Keep of the Castle, where the ceremony of the day took place, was finely and handsomely fitted up, and this, with the large audience and the coloured dresses, etc., etc., made a very fine and imposing spectacle. The Duke and Duchess afterwards visited the Girls' Technical School and School of Cookery on St. George's Plain, and subsequently inspected the Cathedral under the guidance of the Dean. They then returned to Thorpe Station and home to Sandringham. The streets of Norwich were finely decorated, and in the evening there were illuminations.

On the following evening I, with the Mayoress, held a very large reception at the Castle Museum to celebrate the Royal opening. About one thousand guests were present. The Museum rooms throughout, as well as the Grand Keep, were beautifully lighted and decorated; two bands played, and the function was considered to be a very brilliant one. It was, of course, the first gathering of the kind held in the Castle Museum.

The opening of the Castle came at a time when the people of Norwich badly needed something to cheer them up, for unemployment was rife, the weather exceptionally severe and, following a strike in the mines, house coal had become a very expensive commodity. Even worse was the influenza epidemic which raged for months and, at one time, resulted in a weekly mortality rate as high as sixty per thousand.

It must have been with a certain degree of relief that, on

November 9th, 1894, Sir Peter ended his second Mayoralty and handed over to Lieutenant-Colonel Charles Edward Bignold who, twenty years earlier, had succeeded his father, Sir Samuel, at the helm of the Norwich Union Fire Insurance Office. Barely six months later, however, Fate was to deal a cruel blow by the death of Col. Bignold and, under pressure from his peers, Sir Peter reluctantly agreed to take over the Mayoralty for the remainder of the year – his third spell as Mayor of the City.

By this time he had passed his seventieth birthday and, at a special meeting of the Town Council on September 25th, 1895 he was presented with the Honorary Freedom of the City. Then, members of the Corporation and other interested persons made their way to the Castle Museum, where he was presented with a portrait of himself, privately subscribed for and painted by Stanhope Forbes, A.R.A. After having accepted the portrait, he immediately presented it to the Castle Museum, to be hung in its picture gallery – a most appropriate home for it, in view of the part he had played in reclaiming the Castle for the people of Norwich.

"I need hardly say," he wrote, "that this day was one of the most memorable and gratifying to me of my whole life, and was doubtless unique in the history of Norwich".

By 1900 he had practically retired from professional work, but at the end of the year he published his book on "The Norfolk & Norwich Hospital". From then onwards he continued his work for the good of the City and its people, regularly attending civic meetings, as well as events connected with 'his' hospital and 'his' church.

Gradually, however, his diary became less a record of events and more a report of the deaths of so many of the people with whom he had been acquainted. Then, on January 19th, 1911, he began recording his own waning state of health: "I have now completed eighty-six years of life and in many respects I have felt fully a year older than last January, both in physical and mental power". In 1912: "I am sensibly less strong in almost every particular than I was a year ago". In 1913: "I have an increasing sense of the possible contingencies of the incoming years – and well may it be so, for I am only two years off the grand age of ninety". 1914 carried no mention, but on his birthday in 1915 he recorded with pride: "I am ninety years old today, and thus begin to enter my ninety-first year". That was on January 19th, but six

Sir Peter Eade at the age of 90.

months later, on July 19th, the inscription was ominous, for it read: "Up to the spring of this year my general and mental health have been good, but since February I have been much ailing with an acutely dilated heart. The symptoms are very serious, and not improbably imply that my long life is drawing to a close".

That was the final entry in his diary. For the last two or three days of life, he lay in a state of unconsciousness until, on the morning of August 12th, he slipped quietly away.

His funeral service took place on August 16th in his parish church of St. Giles, and then they took him to Blofield Churchyard and laid him to rest with the other six members of his immediate family – his father, his mother and his four sisters.

The high regard in which Sir Peter was held was well reflected in the words of his long-standing friend, Dr. Sydney Long:

> As a colleague for nearly twenty years at the Norfolk and Norwich Hospital, I was privileged to know Sir Peter Eade as intimately, perhaps, as anyone connected with this institution, and a more honourable man and patriotic citizen of Norwich it would be impossible to find.

Lady Eade survived Sir Peter for just a few months. She died in the St. Giles' Street house on June 6th, 1916, and on June 10th she was taken to lie with him at Blofield.

The Great Flood, 1912.

In the last week of August in 1912 the city of Norwich and, indeed, much of Norfolk suffered at the hands of the elements in a deluge of such severity as had never been known before.

It was late afternoon on Sunday, August 25th that black, threatening storm clouds, carried in by ever-strengthening winds, began to appear in the skies above the city. Then, with startling suddenness, the heavens opened up and heavy rain began to fall. Older residents remembered the deluge they had endured in 1878, but the desolation brought about on that occasion was to be as nothing compared with what they were about to undergo. The rain did not cease until the following Wednesday morning, by which time no less than seven inches had fallen, an unprecedented statistic in local weather records.

Not surprisingly, it was the lower lying parts of the city, and especially those near the river, which fared the worst, with the Heigham district and the area around Magdalen Street being badly hit. In almost no time the water was pouring into basements and ground floor rooms, with their occupants obliged to seek safety upstairs. The water in many of the streets soon reached two or three feet in depth, and the only way in which direct contact could be made with those people in the houses was by means of carts or boats.

Trowse, also, was badly affected, as was the whole of the land next to the river by the Cathedral and St. Helen's Hospital, which was completely inundated. At St. Helen's, in fact, the meadow was submerged under four feet of water which spread into one of the inmates' wards and the kitchen, as well as the church and its cloisters. The combination of rain and wind rapidly converted the garden of St. Helen's House into a storm-tossed lake.

The Gas Works, down by the river, and the Electricity Works in Duke Street were partially flooded, and for some two or three days the city's electricity supply was cut off, though fortunately the gas supply never failed.

At the height of the storm, roof tiles and slates were being blown

127

Magdalen Street, Norwich, under flood water, 1912.

Lakenham Bridge.

Trowse Bridge.

Westwick Street, Norwich.

off by the violent winds, and there was hardly a house in the city that escaped damage from either wind or rain.

As soon as the seriousness of the situation became apparent, immediate efforts were made to relieve the suffering of those residents of the city who were most badly affected, and some two thousand men, women and children were rescued from their flooded homes and taken to be cared for by an army of volunteers in higher parts of the city. An appeal for cash assistance was opened by the Lord Mayor, and the sum of £24,000 was immediately forthcoming.

Of course, it was not only the city of Norwich that felt the effects of the storm, for many low-lying areas of the county suffered severely. Great damage was done to standing crops, as well as to roads and bridges. Indeed, no less than 42 bridges over rivers and streams in the county were either severely breached or completely washed away. Also, to add to the dislocation of normal life, many of the telegraph and telephone lines were blown down, most of the rail services were cancelled because of the unsafe condition of the tracks and signals, and postal services were greatly curtailed.

It is not surprising that the Great Flood of 1912 stayed long in the memory of those who lived through it.

September 1st.

A Round on the Links.

All through my life I have managed to resist the efforts of my golfing friends to persuade me to share with them the delights of the game they love. The nearest I ever came to putting club to ball was an hour or so of pitch and putt at Wicksteed Park in Kettering, but that was merely a pleasurable diversion, far removed from teeing off on the first green at Wentworth or Gleneagles.

My disinclination to take up the game did not stem from any dislike of golf, for I know it to be a splendid pastime, and I will readily sit enthralled before a television set and marvel at the uncanny skills of the top international exponents of the sport. No – it was all a question of time, for each of us has a life-span of inescapable brevity which calls for a sorting out of priorities. After all, even a single round of golf takes a fair amount of time; then there is the fact that, if I had taken up the game, I would have wished to strive for some degree of proficiency, and that would have involved a great deal of time-consuming practice. I have sometimes wondered which other facets of my life would have fallen by the wayside if I had succumbed to the blandishments of my golfing friends – a pointless exercise, of course, for everybody's past is liberally sprinkled with 'ifs' and 'buts' and 'might-have-beens'.

Equally inconclusive, yet somehow strangely pleasurable, has been the consideration of which Course would have witnessed my initiation into the sport. If I had gone at the behest of one of my friends, I would probably have been dragged to the one over which he exercised his skills, but that might well have been counter-productive for I have no great love of opulence or grandeur, whether man-made or produced by the hand of Nature. I have often confessed to being more at peace in a village church than a cathedral, more relaxed in a country cottage than a stately home. Much better, I feel, to have chosen one of the eight or nine seaside links dotted around our coastline; but which one would it have been? With little doubt, I feel it could only have been Brancaster.

It was in my 1930s boyhood that I first became acquainted with

Brancaster Lifeboat was an added attraction. This photograph, taken in April 1892, shows the *Alfred S. Genth* on her "Naming Day".

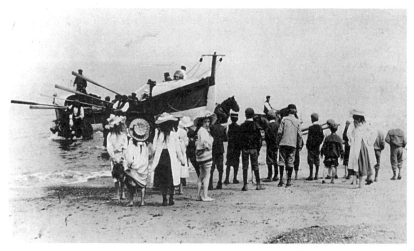

An exercise launch, c.1900. The four horses which pulled the lifeboat down the beach are being ridden back to the shore to await her return.

Brancaster, after previously sampling the attractions of Holkham beach and finding them sadly lacking in appeal. Firstly, there was the fact that, unless one consulted the tide tables in advance, the sea always seemed to be so far out as to be almost invisible. Then there was that huge expanse of sand, so vast and featureless that one's boredom threshold was reached long before the tide decided to come in. At Cromer we had found unflagging interest in the little rocky pools, with starfish left behind by the sea and kittywitches hiding beneath the rocks, but Holkham had none of that – not even seaweed. Then there was the ever-present fear of being trapped by quicksands, like the two nursemaids from Holkham Hall who had suffered that fate and were drowned. No doubt the story had been told to us to ensure that we were aware of possible dangers, for it was many years earlier that the mishap had occurred, but such thoughts are not easily expunged from the mind of a child.

We were never really happy on Holkham beach, but Brancaster, although so close, was a completely different proposition. It was, in short, a paradise of tranquillity, the most delectable of playgrounds, where every turn of the head would bring something different into view.

The land ran down from the sporadically-wooded fields above the village to the greyish-green of the marshes, and then to the pristine sands, pale gold and almost white in stark contrast to the bronze of the mud-flats. Then, stretching as far as the eye could see, there was the matt-blue ocean – there was nothing else, for Brancaster faces due north, with no intervening land-masses to protect it from the winds as they come surging down from the polar regions. But it was summertime when I met Brancaster – the sun shone, the beaches were wide and the swimming was safe.

The same, however, could not be said of Brancaster Marsh, for that was a treacherous area and no place for the unwary. A man-made causeway carried a single road for something like six hundred yards from the village to the shore, with this wetland on either side. The Marsh was often submerged by the spring tides but, when the sea-lavender came into bloom, it became a vision of purple, full of birds giving out their varied calls. There I saw redshank, whimbrel and curlew – at least, that is what a local fisherman told me they were, for I had never seen such birds before, except on cigarette cards.

The natural beauty of that area of wetland, however, is not its greatest attribute, for it has also been the strongest factor in enabling the village to retain its identity. Brancaster Marsh, unstable and precarious, has always deterred developers and saved that precious stretch of foreshore from the fate which has overtaken so many seaside resorts where bricks and mortar, pressing relentlessly forward, could find a secure footing.

Then, of course, there was Brancaster's other attraction – that gently undulating strip of turf, firm and dry, running between the sea and the tidal marshes and giving the distinct impression that Nature had provided it with the sole intent that it should become a golf course. Prior to 1892 it had been common land, with only the traditional villagers having common rights to graze their cattle and ponies there. In that year, however, agreement was reached between the villagers and the residents of the surrounding area that Nature's invitation should be accepted and grazing should give was to golfing. Eighteen holes were laid out, using every inch of the close-cropped turf which years of grazing had produced. Nine holes ran outwards, with the grey-green marsh on the players' right hand, to the ninth green on a little hummock from which they could look across to Scolt Head. Then there were nine holes back, from which they could survey the sea and wave to walkers on the beach.

In return for the loss of their grazing rights, the people of the village acquired the right to play on the course free of charge whilst other residents paid a hefty membership fee for the privilege. Hence there came into being two clubs playing over the same course – the Royal West Norfolk Club and the Brancaster Village Club. Members of the former soon built themselves a sturdy clubhouse of Carr stone and red brick, which the villagers were only allowed to enter by invitation; but they in their turn, were quite content with what one of them described to me as their "little hut". The Royal West Norfolk had its own distinctive flag, so the Village Club followed suit and took great delight in flying theirs during their permitted playing times.

The late Sir Lawrence Jones, a great lover of Brancaster and its golf course, did not exactly approve of the external appearance of the clubhouse. Indeed, he considered it a blot on the landscape, describing it in the most scathing of terms.

"The late Victorians," he wrote, "had a knack of doing unaccountable things. The horizontal lines and quiet undulations of this stretch of coast might have suggested, one would have

The Club House, Brancaster.

The 18th Green, viewed from the Club House balcony.

Dormy House.

thought, a low, long building, crouching to avoid the gales, hugging the marram-grass among the dunes. Instead, a tall, narrow, lop-sided, defiantly hideous object was erected, built of brash red brick, gabled, gawky, dominating and shameless. It was sited on a hump of sand exposed to the attacks of the high tides; it is both a folly and a monstrosity".

Harsh words, indeed, but, even if the Victorians lacked much of an eye for beauty, they did at least understand comfort, and on the north coast of Norfolk there are many months of the year when comfort becomes a main concern. Even Sir Lawrence conceded that point and overcame his dislike of the exterior in favour of the mollifying pleasures to be found within:

"And yet, so strong is the spell of Brancaster, so pleasant were the luncheons in that large, light dining-room on the first floor, so comforting the leather armchairs into which one sank, sighing for toast and tea at the end of an afternoon round, that I recall the building with nothing but affection".

In 1893, a building similar in construction to the clubhouse was erected in the village by the delightfully-named Holcombe Ingleby Esquire and later, in 1929, enlarged to serve the needs of club members and their guests, under the managership of Harry Short.

It was named, in true golfing parlance, the Dormy House Club and was a particularly busy place on Fridays when visiting gentry arrived in their motor cars to use it as their base for a week-end of competitive play. On those occasions, also, local lads of all ages would congregate there in the hope of being engaged for a spot of caddying. There were agreed rates of pay for this task, the smaller boys receiving sixpence per round, rising to as much as 7s. 6d. when they reached the age of 14, and a full ten shillings for men. Many of the youngsters were much more than mere bag-carriers, for they knew every inch of the course, and many became Club members.

Local fisherman Cyril Southerland, who became a member of the Village Club in the early sixties, had earlier seen service as a caddy, and he happily recalls an incident when he was a mere twelve years old. It was a big match, and he duly followed his player until they reached the 13th tee. There was a slight pause, and then the man turned to him and asked which club he should use.

"6-iron," said Cyril.

The man took a 5 and promptly overshot the green.

"I should have taken your advice," he said.

It goes without saying that golf at Brancaster has changed much since the two Clubs came into being over a century ago. There was a time, for instance, when women were by no means welcome, and there are memories of one such lady visitor, barred from entry to the clubhouse, being handed a glass of ginger beer through the open window.

But perhaps the biggest change of all has taken place on the course itself, for it seems that Nature, having provided that stretch of turf in the first place, now wants it back. For many years steady erosion by the sea has been taking place, and in more recent years the ferocity of the elements has wrought havoc, as when, in 1942, the 11th hole was swept away. But, as one member put it, "the sea is gaining ground, but the battle is not yet lost. If the worst comes to the worst, more common land will have to be found to replace what's lost. The West Norfolk and the Village must work together".

Meanwhile, however, the village itself is changing. The fishermen have sadly watched their little cottages being "done up" and everything becoming more expensive. It seems that Brancaster, in common with all the other villages along that stretch of coastline, is paying the penalty for its own great popularity. Nevertheless, whatever the future may bring, memories of golf at Brancaster will never fade, at least as long as there are people to recall them.

There is little doubt that, by common consent, those few sweet years just before the outbreak of the Second World War were the golden age of golf in that tranquil and sequestered spot, for, as with so many other aspects of Norfolk life, things were destined never to be quite the same when the fighting was over. Furthermore, it must be acknowledged that much of the spirit of joy and contentment which pervaded the area stemmed from the "incomers" – the vanguard of the folk who came from other parts to enjoy life in that rural haven. But they came to give as well as to take. They were spirited invaders who brought with them gaiety, wit and, above all, friendliness. They became Brancastrians, and they brought up their offspring in the same mould. The fathers strode over the hallowed turf, hitting golf balls prodigious distances over the marshy inlets. They laughed and gossiped in the clubhouse while the mothers and children built sand castles on the beach and caught shrimps for tea.

One of the first of such people to arrive, and certainly destined to become the figurehead amongst all others, was Major Gilbert Legh, who came from his native Cheshire and took up residence at the Drove House in Thornham. Known to his intimate friends as "Joey" but to the rest simply as "The Major", he was a true character in every sense of the word. Physically he was of diminutive stature, with a number of features which, at first glance, gave him an appearance verging on the comical. There was his fluffy moustache, his monocle and his slightly receding chin, together with a jaunty gait and dainty feet that tended to turn out as he walked, a combination which suggested to some that he could well have stepped out of the pages of *Punch*. Nothing could have been further from the truth, however, for he was a man with great originality of thought, combined with a sense of humour and more than an average share of humanity. He could be dogmatic, but he loved discussion and took great delight in introducing some outrageous idea and then deriding, contradicting and chaffing those who took part in the conversation, always in the most puckish and good-humoured of manners.

The Major drove to his golf at Brancaster in a pony-cart. He played what golfers would call "a short but canny game," paid his caddy the statutory fee and not a penny more, and then drove home to his garden at Thornham. This was the other great love of his life, packed as it was to bursting point with rare trees and shrubs which, said one of his contemporaries, "he loved to caressing point".

For some years he shared his home with Archie and Doris Jamieson, who also became prominent figures in the local scene. Many were the dinner parties at the Drove House, where so many of the new Brancastrians, having fallen under the spell of the place and decided to stay, were pampered and spoilt with the best of everything – not just good food but, as the port circulated, the most stimulating of conversation. Major Legh called everybody "me dear" and was never short of something fresh to discuss.

The pull of Brancaster had an almost magical quality about it, and Major Legh and the Jamiesons were members of a whole colony of new Brancastrians. There were the Harveys and the Gilliats, the Trees, Geoffrey Cory-Wright and his family, and Major Leslie at Appletree Cottage, together with others who have become just ghosts of the past. They were lively and full of vigour, and their offspring took after them. But the War dealt harshly with the younger breed of Brancastrians, for they were of the age to bear its full brunt, and many were destined to be cut down. Yet their memory is still there, in a cluster around the beach huts, young, purposeful and full of a promise that was destined to be unfulfilled.

One of those who, though wounded, survived Hitler's War was Major David Jamieson, son of Archie and Doris, who not only returned to the Drove House, but also brought with him the Victoria Cross, awarded for his actions south of Caen during the liberation of France in August 1944.

It is, I believe, worthy of mention that Major Jamieson later became a Gentleman-at-Arms to the Queen, attending Her Majesty on such State occasions as the Opening of Parliament. Then, on his retirement from that Office, she bestowed upon him the further honour of Commander of the Royal Victorian Order.

"Brancaster," I was told, "could hit back as well as suffer".

The Thorpe Railway Accident.

On the evening of September 10th, 1874, a well-laden passenger train was making its way through wind and rain from Great Yarmouth to Norwich, where it was due to arrive at 9-40. The journey was uneventful as the train pulled punctually into Brundall Station, from where the track became a single line of rails for the last couple of miles into Norwich. At about the same time, a down train from Norwich to London regularly came along that line and passed through Brundall on its way to the capital and, if that express had not cleared the length of single track, it was normal practice for the Yarmouth train to wait in the station until the line ahead was clear.

On this occasion, the stop at Brundall was brief and, though the passengers had not noticed the passing of the London train, the regular travellers among them feared nothing, for they knew that, on occasions when that train was particularly late, it was customary for it to be held in Norwich until the arrival there of the Yarmouth train. Hence, everything seemed normal as their train left Brundall. Everything, indeed, *was* normal until they reached the foot of the Postwick decline, almost opposite the village of Thorpe.

It was there that the two trains, both travelling at something like thirty miles an hour, met in head-on collision. A sudden shock went through the Yarmouth train, followed immediately by the sound of a sharp metallic concussion. Both trains, with many of the carriages smashed almost beyond recognition, came to a halt spread-eagled across the track and onto the adjacent meadows. In and around the carriages, 27 passengers lay dead and another seventy or eighty injured, many with limb fractures. Small wonder that the tragedy of that night became known as the Great Thorpe Accident.

It so happened that four medical men were travelling on the Yarmouth train, one of whom, Mr. Bransby Francis, was fatally injured. One of the others, however, was able to give a vivid eye-witness account of the happenings of that night.

"Immediately upon the shock," he wrote, "I felt that my carriage had come to a sudden standstill; then the compartment in which I was sitting seemed to diminish itself in its dimensions, at the same time as the carriage turned sideways. Then I knew no more until I picked myself up from the wet grass of a meadow, into which I suppose I had been thrown. I collected myself together and was able to appreciate at once that the night was dark, that rain was falling fast, and that steam was roaring from the funnel of an engine, which was standing in dangerous proximity to my person".

As soon as he had recovered from his fall and realised that he had not received any mortal injury, he went and spoke to the less fortunate passengers, some unable to extricate themselves from the shattered carriages, and others lying on the sides of the small embankment.

"It was at once all too evident that the injuries were numerous and severe. Many were crying out for help, two or three more were sitting on the cold, wet earth, moaning and nursing their broken limbs. But, as my head was bleeding, my face covered with dust and dirt, my cap gone, my coat torn and my whole body feeling the effect of nervous excitement and shock, I gladly accepted the offer of a kind friend to go to his house close by and wash and take some brandy, after which I returned to give what help I could to the injured".

The scene at the 'Tuns' public house, whose occupants offered such aid as they were able to give, resembled the base hospital of a battlefield, with many of the inhabitants of Thorpe dashing from their homes to offer assistance. But, with nothing other than broken sticks for splints and torn-up towels for bandages, there was little that even the doctor could do. It was nearly an hour before further, and more welcome, aid arrived from Norwich with appliances for the broken limbs, and with carriages in which the injured could be taken to hospital or to their homes.

In the aftermath of the disaster, there was much discussion as to its cause. *The Times,* which gave the story much coverage, rather verbosely pronounced that "the radical error was the unpunctuality of the trains, with the consequent necessity for varying the arrangements on the single line, and the necessary dependence, therefore, of safety upon the accuracy of individuals, or the exact carrying out of orders, which have varied from day to day according to the varying circumstances".

Or, rather more simply, 'human error'.

October 12th.

Murder Most Foul.

Some years ago I visited an elderly Norwich lady of my acquaintance and, as we talked, her thoughts went back to her earlier life, and she recalled a period when she had suffered from a slight, but none the less painful, medical condition. It seems she had developed a bunion which had become infected and needed frequent attention, carried out by the local nurse who called on alternate days to change the dressing.

One day, however, it was a different nurse who visited her and, when asked if she was taking over from her predecessor, she replied, "Oh, no. I'm on holiday and just helping out. I'm going back to my hospital in Belgium tomorrow". The year was 1914 and German armies were already rampaging through Europe. My friend was horrified.

"You can't possibly go there," she said. "It's so dangerous".

"I *must* go back," said the nurse. "My work is there".

The nurse was Edith Cavell, little known at that time, but destined, all too soon, to become immortalised throughout the free world.

Edith Cavell was born on December 4th, 1865, in an old-fashioned house on the Green at the Norfolk village of Swardeston. Then, when she was about three years old, the family moved into the new vicarage by the church, of which her father was vicar for 46 years and where he now sleeps with his wife in eternal rest. The little girl was brought up upon the strictest Victorian principles of service before self and, when she was twenty-two, she became a nurse, a calling to which she was to devote her entire life.

I have no knowledge of how she originally came to find herself in Belgium, but it was there, in a single room in Brussels, that she founded a little hospital known as L'Ecole Infirmière Belge. Over the years her little hospital grew to become a vast building with a large staff of nurses, and it was in 1906, when she was 41, that it became known as the Berkendael Medical Institute, with herself installed as Matron.

Nurse Edith Cavell.

On the outbreak of war, as danger threatened, she could quite easily have forsaken her hospital and sought the safety of her homeland. Indeed, on the very day that hostilities began she was actually on leave, staying with her mother in Norwich, and she could easily have chosen to stay. But tending the sick was her sole reason for living and, even when Belgium was overcome by the Prussian hordes, she did not falter. She continued to give succour not only to Belgian and British soldiers, but also to wounded Germans, for nursing knows no boundaries. Soon, however, the invaders became suspicious of her activities and they searched her hospital for anything which might support their belief that she was helping Allied soldiers to escape to Holland.

On August 5th, 1915 they arrested her and charged her with aiding the escape of "enemy" soldiers. Her trial by court martial took place on October 7th, and the German High Command, deaf to the protests of the ambassadors of neutral nations, sentenced her to death. Five days later, under cover of darkness on the night of October 12th, she was led into a garden and shot.

The shot rang round the world and filled the hearts of free men and women with both pity and revulsion, but nowhere were those feelings felt more strongly than in Nurse Cavell's home country. "MURDER MOST FOUL!" was the banner headline in the *Daily Sketch,* and that newspaper's leading article echoed the feelings of its readers:

"Consider the crime charged against this noble woman. Germany breaks into a neutral nation with iron and fire. Instantly patriotism in that country becomes, in the Prussian code, a crime. To succour or shelter the wounded of your own people is punishable by death. You must put aside all natural affection; you must become the slave and the spy of your master from Berlin, or your breast will be shattered with bullets, though you be a woman. This action had the true German touch, for it was blood that was lusted for. That is the system which Germany not only endures but would enforce on the free peoples".

Another writer declared: "Men of England will sing no hymn of hate, but they will hear the pistol shot ringing out at the dead of night, and that pistol shot not only slew one of the tenderest of women, but it is the signal to other women to send their sons, and to the shirker of yesterday to take his share in the victory that is to be".

The King addressed an appeal to the men: "The end is not in

A woman billposter, taking the place of a man at the Front, sticks up
exhortations to the men of Thetford to join him, 1916.
The lady here is John Clarke's daughter Florrie who, while her father was
away at War, also took over his duties as Town Crier.

sight. More men and yet more are needed to keep my Armies in the field..."

Edith Cavell's sister, Florrie, Matron of the Hull and East Riding Sanatorium and Convalescent Home in Withernsea, near Hull, added her appeal:

"Tell the young men who have not responded that now is their time. Surely my sister's sad end will move them to heed the call. If only they will roll up I know my sister will not have died in vain. And something tells me they will roll up".

A rhymester of the time put it slightly differently:

> Prompted by a life's devotion,
> Death she met, unmoved by fears.
> Men of England! Quell emotion.
> Join! Become her Cavell-iers.

The result was a tremendous surge of men queuing up to join the Army. On the day after her execution, the *Daily Sketch* sent a correspondent to Nurse Cavell's home village, from where he reported that "Swardeston has soon given its verdict on her martyrdom, for already several score young fellows have enlisted". The action of the German High Command on that wretched night may well have been their greatest mistake of the entire war. It was a hideous act of sheer, utter vengeance, for they could gain nothing by taking the life of that dedicated angel of mercy, whose sole object in life was the relief of suffering. To the peoples of the free world, however, it brought an even stronger conviction that the Kaiser and his henchmen must, once and for all, be made to pay for their crimes against humanity.

The greatest sadness felt by the British people after Nurse Cavell's death stemmed, perhaps, from the fact that, throughout her ordeal, she stood alone. There was no friend to stand by her at her trial; nobody to speak in her defence. Her only comfort came from the Reverend Stirling Gahan, the English Chaplain in Brussels, and it was to him that she spoke those last words which forever fill the heart of every Norfolk man and woman with pride:

I am not afraid or apprehensive. I have seen death so often that it does not seem to me strange or terrible. I thank God for these ten weeks of rest before the end. Life has always been troubled and full of problems: this time of rest has been very welcome. Every one about me

The funeral cortège arrives at the Erpingham Gate.

has been very good to me, but I want to say, now that I
face God and eternity, that I realise that patriotism is
not enough; I must have no hatred or bitterness toward
anyone.

After the war, Nurse Cavell's body was brought back to England and given a funeral service of almost royal proportions in Westminster Abbey. From there she made her last journey by train to Norwich, where crowds lined the streets as her coffin made its way on a gun carriage along Prince of Wales Road, round the corner into Tombland, and finally through the Erpingham Gate into the peace of the Cathedral Close. Girl Guides saluted and nurses and local citizens stood in silence as the coffin was carried on the shoulders of six Norfolk soldiers to Life's Green, the secluded retreat around the eastern side of the Cathedral where birds sing and the city is lost to sight. There, far from strife and bitterness, and in the shadow of the chapel dedicated to those who died for us in the Great War, Edith Cavell at last reached her final resting place.

The Norwich memorial to Nurse Cavell, originally outside the Nursing Association premises on Tombland, but now in the shelter of the wall near the Erpingham Gate.

The memorial erected by the Belgians outside her hospital in Brussels, November 22nd, 1918.

A Patriot, 1915.

Oh tell it not in whispers,
    But shout it far and wide,
How that noble English woman,
    Nurse Edith Cavell died.

Tell it to the children,
    By the fireside's cheerful glow,
When they ask you for a story
    Of the days of long ago.

Tell them how this Norfolk woman
    Tended friend and foe as well;
And because she did her duty,
    By a coward's hand she fell.

Tell them how a thrill of horror
    Was sped throughout our clime;
And men flocked to join the army
    to avenge so foul a crime.

And that now throughout the Empire,
    Wherever they shall travel,
There is told the noble story
    Of the death of brave Nurse Cavell.

Lucilla Reeve.

Sir Thomas Browne.

On October 19th, 1905, a large group of civic dignitaries, together with a number of distinguished visitors and several hundred onlookers, gathered on Norwich's Haymarket for the ceremonial unveiling of a statue of Sir Thomas Browne. It has always seemed strange to me that the City should have left it so long before thus honouring its illustrious former citizen for, by the time they got round to it, he had been dead for well over two centuries. But, of course, Norwich folk have never been ones to clutter up their streets and open spaces with statues. Wander the city as you will, and you will need no more than the fingers of one hand to count them.

Perhaps it was also a slight feeling of guilt that brought about the erection of the memorial to Sir Thomas, for, even today, many people have never heard of him and, of those who have, quite a few simply know that he wrote a book called *Religio Medici*. There was much more to the man than that, however, and the late R.H. Mottram – who knew more than most about such things – said of him: "He remains today one of the most deservedly famous of all the sons and daughters of Norwich whom one picks out, if asked to name a dozen such".

He lived in Norwich from 1636 until his death in 1682 and was one of the grandees of those times. He was, it is true, a landowner, but his real eminence stemmed from his professional status, for he was one of the first men to become a real Doctor of Medicine rather than a mere blood-letter or apothecary. Much more to the point, however, is the fact that, when Norwich became the centre of Oliver Cromwell's Eastern Association, he remained loyal to the King. Yet he was never threatened by events around him – a sure sign of his local prestige. It is little wonder, perhaps, that Charles the Second, on his ceremonial visit to Norwich in 1671, should have bestowed a knighthood upon him in the 'New Hall', now known to us as Blackfriars' Hall.

Sir Thomas Browne was a big family man – in more ways than one, for his loving wife, Lady Dorothy, begat him nine daughters "as well as a son or two". They lived in a rather stately house which stood, until midway through the nineteenth century, on the corner of Orford Place, just in front of the Lamb Inn. There it was that he wrote his most renowned book, *Religio Medici,* as well as such lesser works as *Garden of Cyprus, Christian Morals, Common Errors* and *Urn Burial.* It was there, also, that he entertained learned men from all over England, for he was nationally renowned as a great man of learning.

There is little doubt that, if the house was still in existence, it would be revered as a great civic treasure. It was the Victorians, however, who demolished it and erected, in its place, one in their own particular style which they named Orford Chambers. They did, at least, adorn it with a plaster panel with an inscription informing passers by that 'on this site lived Sir Thomas Browne, M.D., author of *Religio Medici.*' With, perhaps, more good luck than forethought, a splendid timber mantelpiece from the house, elaborately carved and inset with semi-precious stone, found itself, after many wanderings, within the safety of the Castle Museum.

There was one part of Sir Thomas Browne's property which was to outlive the remainder by more than a century, and that was his Garden House, with its famous, richly-ornamented ceiling. This was to become the property of George Green when, at the beginning of this century, he opened his renowned outfitting business facing the Haymarket. He did not incorporate it into his new building, but chose to call it the Livingstone Hotel and put it to the use of his commercial representatives and their stock. There it stood until 1960 when, together with Green's store, it was demolished to make way for a more modern commercial retail outlet. Nobody, it seems, realised the significance of the old building with its magnificent ceiling. An acquaintance of mine, involved in the clearance of the site, recently recalled to me his memory of the "old, timbered, Elizabethan-looking building, standing out at the back". I count myself fortunate to have the memory of just one boyhood visit to the building – and a photograph to remind me of the treasure which the City threw away in 1960.

Sir Thomas Browne, philosopher, physician, collector and writer, died in 1682 and was buried in his Parish Church of St. Peter Mancroft – at least, most of him was. During the research for his book on Urn Burials, he became only too well aware of the grave-robbing which occurred in earlier times and was thus

Sir Thomas Browne's house, Haymarket, Norwich. Demolished 1842.

The Livingstone Hotel, formerly Sir Thomas Browne's Garden House.
Demolished 1960.

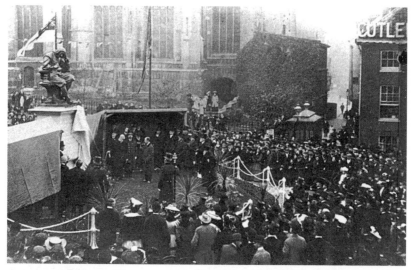
The unveiling ceremony, Hay Hill. October 19th, 1905.

moved to write: "To be knaved out of our graves, to have our skulls made drinking bowls and our bones turned into pipes, are tragical abominations escaped by burning burials". How ironic that he should have been "knaved out of his grave" and his skull sold to a Norwich doctor, then to be kept in the museum of a local hospital until its retrieval and restoration to its proper place in 1922.

On his death, Lady Dorothy, his wife for 41 years, set up a memorial bearing his coat of arms in the chancel of St. Peter's. There also, in the sacristy, is a plaster cast of his skull, together with the shield-shaped brass plate from his coffin and what is said to be one of the best existing portraits of him, painted soon after he received his knighthood.

That, then, was the man who, so many years later, the City Fathers and their guests gathered together to honour. The bronze figure, mounted on a granite pedestal bearing a suitable inscription, represents Sir Thomas Browne in a sitting position contemplating a broken urn – though there are some who, erroneously, believe it to be a skull! The work was executed by Henry Pegram, A.R.A., and the cost was met by public subscription, with donations being received from all over the world. The statue was erected in the centre of Hay Hill and was surrounded by a garden, with close-cropped grass, flower beds and

154

Sir Thomas Browne's statue, surrounded by flower borders and grass.
Green's outfitting shop is in the background and the
Haymarket Picture House on the right.

trees.

The unveiling ceremony was carried out by Lord Avebury (formerly Sir John Lubbock) in the presence of a highly distinguished gathering. There were deputations from the Royal Colleges of Physicians and Surgeons; there were Dr. Clifford Allbutt and Dr. Osler, Regius Professors of Medicine at the Universities of Cambridge and Oxford respectively; and, of course, the Mayor, Sheriff and Corporation. After the ceremony, the Committee who had organised the occasion entertained about 130 subscribers to lunch in Blackfriars' Hall, and in the evening a memorial service was held in St. Peter Mancroft Church, with the sermon being preached by Bishop Mitchinson, Master of Pembroke College, Oxford, where Sir Thomas Browne was educated.

Some time later, Mr. Pegram produced a small model of the statue, also in bronze and measuring about eighteen inches in height. One copy of this was presented to the Royal College of Physicians in London, a second went to Professor Osler at Oxford, and the final copy to Mr. F.R. Eaton who, as Secretary to the Committee, had done such sterling work in raising the necessary funds for the memorial.

The transformation to Hay Hill brought about by the erection of the statue served a dual purpose for, whilst honouring its former son, it also provided the City with an almost rural oasis of tranquillity. Sadly, the demands of a modern age have swept away the gardens and the trees, pushed Sir Thomas into a corner, and given way to a sea of concrete where passers-by may sit and eat their ice cream and their sandwiches. But at least, in doing so, they have moved him a few yards closer to his final resting place.

October 21st.

Our Proudest Boast.

Trafalgar Day will never be forgotten as long as we have a Navy, but I often wonder whether Norfolk pays due homage to its greatest son. It may be true that he blotted his copybook to some extent with his passion for Lady Hamilton and his parting from his wife, but that could all be forgiven when Horatio Nelson, "Our Hero of the Nile", finally gave his life in sweeping the French and Spanish fleets from the sea off Cape Trafalgar on October 21st, 1805.

Many biographies of the man have been written, some of them in more recent times apparently with the sole objective of trying to "knock him off his pedestal". I can only refer such writers to the time, just one hour before the opposing lines of ships were expected to converge at Trafalgar, when Nelson retired to the comparative peace of his cabin. There Pasco, the flag-lieutenant of *H.M.S. Victory,* coming in with a message, found him on his knees composing the prayer which was part of his legacy to England:

May the Great God whom I worship grant to my Country, and for the benefit of Europe in general, a great and glorious Victory, and may no misconduct in any one tarnish it; and may humanity after Victory be the predominant feature in the British Fleet. For myself, individually, I commit my life to Him who made me, and may His blessing light upon my endeavours for serving my Country faithfully. To Him I resign myself and the just cause which is entrusted to me to defend.

Later, as he lay below, mortally wounded, he begged Hardy, his Captain and great friend, not to throw his body overboard. It was then that, "with some flash of childhood's tenderness battling against the delirium of pain," he asked Hardy to kiss him.

"Thank God I have done my duty," he said, and, as the last ships of the enemy fleets either surrendered or fled to safety, his last words were, "God and my Country". Then, his spirit left his body and "became one with England and the sea".

At this point, without shame, I plead guilty to three counts of bias in my admiration for the man. Firstly, I am a man of Norfolk and, as such, I feel it my bounden duty to honour all that is good in our past history. Then there is the fact that I spent much of the Second World War in the Royal Navy, and I quickly discovered how much of Naval tradition arose through the activities of Admiral Nelson. Look at the Naval salute, for instance. In other Services the salute is carried out with much exertion ("the longest way up and the shortest way down," they used to say) and with the flat palm of the hand facing directly forward. The Naval version, however, is a much more casual affair – and with the hand turned slightly inwards to conceal the palm from view. This is all because of Lady Hamilton, who visited Nelson's ship on an occasion when the crew were caulking the deck and expressed her displeasure at all those pitch-stained palms facing her. Nelson, ever eager to please his paramour, at once decreed that, henceforth, the salute should be carried out with the palm turned inwards. And the Navy has done it that way ever since.

Then there is the fact that the Navy is the only Service in which its officers may remain seated for the Loyal Toast to the Sovereign. This also stems from Nelson's time for, as anybody who has done the tour of *H.M.S. Victory* will realise, the deckheads (in other words, the ceilings) were so low that the necessity for suddenly having to stand erect carried with it the ever-present danger of knocking themselves unconscious.

During my time in the Service, I frequently took great delight in telling my fellow officers that Lord Nelson and I had attended the same school, albeit with the small matter of 167 years between us. I invariably found them an eager audience, for the fact that *Victory* is now permanently moored in the Naval Dockyard at Portsmouth does tend to suggest that Horatio was, perhaps, a Hampshire man. Hence their surprise at learning that the admiral, like their own dental officer, had once been a young Norfolk lad.

Here I must plead guilty to my third charge of bias, brought about by our both being Old Pastonians. I feel such bias to be perfectly acceptable, however, for, as with the Royal Navy, it was impossible to be educated at Sir William Paston's School in North Walsham without absorbing something of the Nelson spirit. That spirit, indeed, was all around us, together with more tangible reminders of the illustrious Old Boy. There was, to begin with, the old School House containing the room in which, just a few

Lord Nelson – Old Pastonians' "Proudest Boast".

NORTH WALSHAM GRAMMAR SCHOOL

The Paston School as Nelson knew it.

The schoolroom in which he received his education.

yards from the fireplace, Nelson sat at his lessons. Then there was his wooden pencil box, a rather plain affair, but bearing a brass plate with the inscription:

Box used by
Horatio Nelson
at his School
at North Walsham
Norfolk, 1770

Sceptics may scoff and query the authenticity of the box, but its history is well documented. The original owner, indeed, was none other than Nelson's great friend and shipmate, Captain Thomas Masterman Hardy, R.N., who, it is thought, had the brass plate affixed to it. It was bequeathed by him to John Hardy, who left it to his great-granddaughter, Miss Pamela Hardy. She in turn sold it to a Mr. Hubert Palmer of Eastbourne, a collector who, a few years later, offered it for sale with a quantity of other Nelson memorabilia. When the sale was announced, to take place at Christie's, it was the first time the School had heard of the existence of the box – and the School promptly bought it. The year was 1932, the very year in which I made my first entry into Paston, and I can still recall the great feeling of history that I experienced when I was allowed to hold it briefly in my excited little hands.

The other tangible reminder of Horatio Nelson was a brick into which he had engraved the initials "H.N.", probably in 1770. It was part of the wall which stood with a row of very fine poplar trees along the eastern end of the playground. When the former pupil achieved fame it became known as "Nelson's Brick" yet, strangely enough, it was left in place and eventually almost forgotten. It was, in fact, a century later that it was rediscovered and promptly placed in a glass case in the old School House.

It was in 1881 and there had been a very severe storm which had blown down a number of the poplars, as well as causing damage to the wall. The damage, in fact, was such that the School had three days holiday in order to clear it up. Just at that time an Old Pastonian named William Rider Haggard went over to visit the School from his home at Bradenham Hall, accompanied by his son, Henry, afterwards renowned as Sir Henry Rider Haggard. The father recalled the brick, which he had known in his schooldays sixty years previously, and decided to search for it. It was an autumn evening and the light was fading, so the search was carried

Horatio Nelson's Pencil Box.

out by the light of a lantern. The brick was found, having narrowly escaped destruction during the storm, for a tree had fallen at that very point. The story of the search was later recorded by Rider Haggard in *The Farmer's Year.*

It was in 1768 that Horatio Nelson entered the Paston School, together with his older brother, William, both of them having previously been pupils at King Edward VI School at Norwich for a short time. Horatio was destined to join the Navy in 1771, but William stayed for a further three years before entering the Church and eventually becoming a Prebendary of Canterbury Cathedral. The two boys were inseparable companions, and their enforced parting on a dark spring morning in 1771 was understandably an occasion of highly charged emotion.

It cannot be said that Horatio, in his early years, showed any physical signs of becoming a Naval hero, for he was slight of build, pale of complexion and, according to some books, subject to "the ague". The veracity of that last statement may be open to some doubt, but one undeniable fact is that, like most of the other boys, he did on one occasion go down with measles. He was nursed through his illness by a certain Miss Gaze (late Mrs. Crosswell), daughter of the parish clerk of North Walsham, and that dear lady was greatly revered in later years by her grandchildren when she recounted the story of how she restored to full health the future hero of England.

Any physical deficiency, however, was more than eclipsed in other ways, for, even at that early age, he showed obvious signs of the courage and leadership which were to be the hallmarks of his later career. There is, for instance, the story of the Master's pears, which has long been part of Paston School folklore.

The Master at that time was the Rev. John Price Jones, a fiery Welshman known to the boys as a "merciless flogger" whilst at the same time being a teacher of great talent – at least for a few years, after which he fell from grace and left Paston in a manner which can only be described as "by mutual agreement". At the time in question, a pear tree in his garden was bearing some exceptionally fine fruit, upon which his scholars cast covetous eyes. Any attempt to gather them, however, was regarded by the boys as being so hazardous that not one of them would undertake the task. It was then that Horatio, seeing his companions' reluctance, came forward and offered to brave the danger. Accordingly, under the cover of darkness, he was lowered down from the dormitory window by means of some sheets tied together "and thus, at a considerable risk, secured the prize". Then, on being hauled up again into the dormitory, he proceeded to share the pears among his schoolfellows, keeping none for himself. It was simply the challenge that had appealed to him and, as he said, "I only took them because every other boy was afraid". The next morning, an irate Mr. Jones offered a reward of five guineas to anybody who would reveal the identity of the plunderer but, in the words of a contemporary, "young Nelson was too much beloved for any boy to betray him".

Young Horatio's bravery that night was to be echoed on that Spring day in 1771 when he became a midshipman on board the *Raisonnable,* under the command of his uncle, Captain Suckling. There can be no doubt that the uncle beheld his nephew with much misgiving, for there was nothing about the young lad (he was only twelve years old) which suggested that he could survive the rigours of life at sea. The Captain decreed that nobody should know of the family relationship between himself and the midshipman and, furthermore, he warned the boy that he could expect no favours because of that relationship. To emphasise this statement, he pointed his finger aloft towards the top of the mainmast and said, "Now, if I were to tell you to climb up to the top of that, would you do it, or would you be frightened?"

There was a slight pause, and back came the reply: "I would be frightened, sir". Another brief pause followed, and then he added, "But I would do it".

"Alright," said the Captain. "Do it!"

And Horatio did it, just as he had climbed down from the dormitory window at Paston when all the others stood back in fear.

The boy became the man, and it was of that man that the noted historian, Sir Arthur Bryant, was moved to write:

"Without influence he had risen by sheer merit to the rank of post-captain before he was twenty-one. He impressed everyone with whom he came into contact professionally with the sense that he was no common being. But his greatest success was with those under his command. He was a man who led by love and example. There was nothing he would not do for those who served under him. There was nothing they would not dare for Nelson".

He was the man of whom generations of Pastonians sang, in the words of their School Song:

> 'Twere long to tell of all who came.
>   Of Woodhouse, Wharton, Hoste;
> Their names are on the roll of fame,
>   And never shall be lost.
> But stand and shout as the last we bring:
> Horatio Nelson – of him we sing,
>   For he is our proudest boast!

October 25th.

To See the King.

So-called "public figures" of today have become infinitely more public than they were in our grandparents' time, with television and newspapers incessantly feeding us with even the most intimate details of their lives. This is particularly true in the case of Royalty, who are now portrayed as human beings, with all the faults and foibles of the rest of us, rather than mysterious beings to be revered from afar. Modern travel, furthermore, brings them constantly into our direct view, but for our grandparents to actually see their King was the experience of a lifetime.

Hence, Monday October 25th, 1909 was a very special day for the citizens of Norwich, for it was then that they received a State Visit from their Sovereign, King Edward VII. He had been staying at Quidenham Hall as the guest of Lord and Lady Albemarle, and it was from there that he and his party, in a convoy of five cars, made their way through the gaily-decorated streets of Attleborough and Wymondham to enter the city at Eaton. There was a brief civic reception at St. Andrew's Hall, after which the King left in a four-horse open landau for the Cavalry Drill Ground at Mousehold, where he was "to review and to present Guidons and Colours to certain units of the Territorial Forces in Norfolk".

The sight which greeted him as his carriage approached St. James' Hill must have warmed his heart, for there, on those gentle slopes, stood a vast assembly of local people, including no less than 11,000 schoolchildren who, having rehearsed well on the previous day, sang the National Anthem as he passed by, each being later rewarded with a bag containing a bun, a meat pie and a banana.

After the military ceremony there was lunch for the King at the Drill Hall in Chapel Field, and then he was off to lay the foundation stone of the forthcoming extensions to the Norfolk and Norwich Hospital. Tea was taken at Crown Point with Mr. and Mrs. Russell Colman, after which His Majesty left the city, "by motor", for Newmarket.

By today's standards it was just a routine Royal visit – but, for our grandparents, a memory to be cherished for a lifetime.

King Edward VII leaving the Drill Hall, October 25th, 1909.

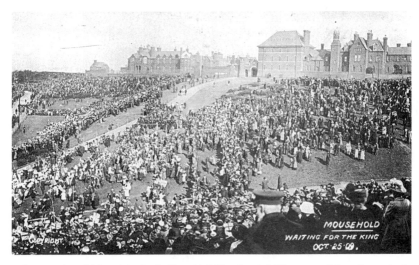

The people of Norwich, including 11,000 schoolchildren, awaiting the arrival of the King on St. James' Hill.

October 26th.

The Abbey Church.

I stood in the Church in the twilight,
In the evening dim and grey,
And in fancy I heard the Curfew ring
The knell of parting day.
I lifted my eyes to the oaken roof,
Fading away in the gloom;
I dropped them again, and they rested
On many an ancient tomb.

I watched the creeping shadows
The great stone pillars cast,
And my mind wandered back from the present
And dwelt on the distant past.
What changes these stones must have witnessed
As the years rolled on and on!
Oh, if only they could speak to us
Of the ages past and gone!

How many lives had been started
At that great white font of stone!
And on – till that life was ended –
At rest in the vaults, alone.
Ages and ages and ages,
Watching a nation's life –
Ages of peace and plenty,
Ages of war and strife.

In fancy I heard from the shadows
Whisperings soft and low;
The Church seemed filled with shadowy forms –
Spectres of long ago.
The grey clad monks and friars,
The silent, shrouded nuns,
The scented, lace-decked cavaliers,
And Cromwell's puritans.

Wymondham Abbey Church, the source of inspiration for Miss Chatterton's poem.

A warrior's mail-clad figure,
A stately, haughty dame;
The havoc-working soldiers
Of King Charles' troubled reign;
The wild and haggard fugitive,
The beggars round the door;
Spectres from the ages,
From the ages gone before.

As I stood there in the silence,
As the shadows round me fell,
I thought – if these walls could only speak –
If they could only tell!
And everything seemed so little –
These few small years of mine –
Just a drop in the ocean,
A stitch in the hem of time!

Una Chatterton. October 26th, 1914

169

Mistress of the Hounds.

A hunting-and-shooting contributor to *The Queen* magazine in 1935 expressed his conviction that "In these vulgar days of scurry and decreasing privacy there is far too much prying into the private lives of public or quasi-public people".

"Nevertheless," he continued, "one occasionally meets an individual, perhaps little known to the world at large, whose mode of living or whose instinct for getting to the root of life constitutes an impressive example to people in general".

The subject of his attention was Sybil Harker, now probably best remembered in her native Norfolk as one-time Master of the Norwich Staghounds.

"Here is a young lady," he wrote, "as pretty as she is charming and as graceful as she is unaffected, not a day older or younger than she looks, who displays characteristics unusual in most of the young women of this heedless age". It was a glowing tribute, echoed by an elderly acquaintance of mine, who described her, rather more succinctly, as "a dashed attractive young filly".

Sybil Harker was a member of the Royal Geographical Society but, unlike many of her fellow-members, she was not content to learn of other countries simply from that Society's magazine, splendid though it was. She travelled widely all around the globe, always regarding the world as an education rather than a picture gallery.

She hunted over the wire-protected countryside of New Zealand with the Bay of Plenty Hounds; she camped among the aborigines of Central Australia; she visited Oregon for the sole purpose of experiencing the lifestyle of its cowboys. She visited the Lapps above the Arctic Circle in Swedish Lapland; she went on a two-week pony trek in Iceland; and, for her, the mountains of Sumatra were not to be admired from the deck of a luxury liner or from the leisured ease of a bungalow verandah, but rather to be climbed, one by one, on the back of one of the island's ponies.

Of course, if one wishes to indulge in such a lifestyle, it is a great advantage to be born into a well-to-do family, and Sybil

Sybil Harker with Donovan, winner of four firsts at the Royal Show, 1934.

Harker lacked nothing in that respect. Her father was Major William Harker of Blofield Hall, High Sheriff of Norfolk; her mother was Mrs. Margaret Gordon Harker, youngest daughter of the renowned Coats family of Paisley.

More important than mere cash, however, are the intangible gifts which can pass from parent to child, and it was from her mother that Sybil Harker inherited the inspiration of service to the community. Her parents had taken up residence at the Hall in 1905, and her mother, in particular, soon became identified with every social activity and personally knew every villager. In 1925, a village hall was required, so she provided it. She started a babies' welfare clinic and arranged for the transport of people from outlying areas. She was president of the District Nursing Association and was the originator of the Linen Guild at the Jenny Lind Hospital. She was a Justice of the Peace for the Blofield Division, a prison visitor and a regular worshipper at the parish church – and she somehow found time to bring four daughters into the world.

Her greatest legacy, however, was her work for the British Red Cross Society, in which her genius for organisation put Norfolk in the forefront of the Society's work. She had joined the Society in 1910, forming a detachment in the village, and the outbreak of the Great War found her opening a war hospital at Brundall House and training reserve detachments of nurses to serve in military hospitals at home and overseas. In recognition of her services she was made Assistant County Director in 1917 and the end of the war saw no abatement in her enthusiasm for the cause. In 1926 she became County Director, a position which she used to further the work of the Society in every possible field, not least in the opening of the Red Cross Dressing Station at Yarmouth, where the Scotch fisher girls received expert treatment for the injuries they received at their work.

After her death on January 14th, 1935, subscription funds were opened to provide suitable memorials to her life of service, with a dedication service in Norwich Cathedral marking the installation of a carved oak lectern in St. Saviour's War Memorial Chapel. Most splendid of all, however, must surely have been the stained glass windows illustrating the varied work of the Red Cross Society, installed in Blofield Church and dedicated by the Bishop of Norwich on October 11th, 1936.

With a maternal example of that nature, it is not surprising that

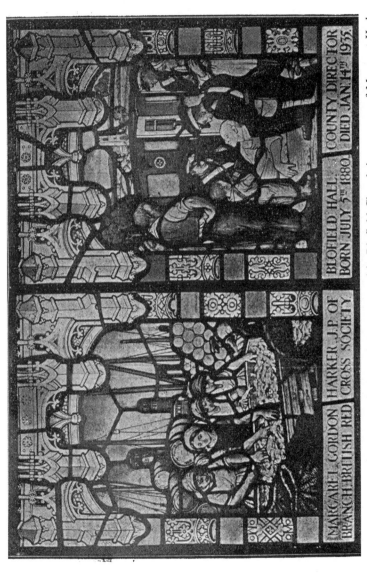

Two of the bottom lights of the stained glass windows erected in Blofield Church in memory of Margaret Harker, 1936. The six windows illustrate the work of the Red Cross Society, including the Dressing Station for the Scotch fisher girls at Yarmouth.

Sybil Harker should dedicate much of her life to what are conveniently called "good causes". She never took unto herself a husband – the nearest she came to a nuptial state was when, in 1932, she was bridesmaid to her sister, Sylvia, on her marriage to Captain Bevan of the Coldstream Guards. It was inevitably a grand social occasion, with something like five hundred invited guests, and a huge crowd of onlookers occupying every vantage point long before the time of the ceremony, their eyes cast upwards at the grey sky lest rain should fall on the red carpet which stretched from the stone porch to the churchyard gate. Both the A.A. and the R.A.C. provided men to marshal the traffic whilst, with revealing frankness, the *Eastern Daily Press* published a complete list of the wedding presents in four and a half columns of tightly packed type.

Sybil, however, was destined to remain a bachelor girl and, to this end, she took up residence at Wacton House, just a mile or so from Long Stratton. Once there, except when she was away on her overseas adventures, she did all that was expected of the Lady of the Manor – and much more besides. She served on parish, district and county councils and on the bench of magistrates which used to meet at Long Stratton. For 24 years she was Chairman of the Governors at Long Stratton High School, as well as being a governor at several other local schools. Following in her mother's footsteps, she became deputy president of the British Red Cross Norfolk branch as well as District Commissioner of the Girl Guides. During the war she was an A.T.S. commander with responsibility for the welfare of evacuees. She cared for both old and young, organising parties for elderly and handicapped people and opening her home for all manner of events. It was in this branch of her work, furthermore, that Miss Harker's never-failing generosity became apparent, for it was sizeable financial donations from her which saw the establishment of Harker House home for the elderly at Long Stratton and the swimming pool at the High School.

Hers was indeed a full life, yet her one great over-riding passion was her love of horses and hounds. She had been born to the saddle and had a long association with the Dunston Harriers. The happiest moment of her life, however, came on the day in 1933 when they made her Master of the Norwich Staghounds, a hunt which had long held a proud position in Norfolk hunting history. She threw herself wholeheartedly into her Mastership with a total dedication

Capt. Tom Thackeray, Huntsman, mounted on Flash, with the bitch pack of Norwich Staghounds, 1935.

to both horses and hounds which drew approval even from those of us who are not greatly enamoured with the idea of chasing animals across the Norfolk countryside. She even went to the length of paying farmers to cut their hedges to a height which her horses could readily jump.

The pack consisted partly of home-bred hounds, together with others brought in from other Hunts – the Bicester, the Belvoir, the Essex and Suffolk and the Sussex Draghounds. The total complement comprised 24 "couple" of hounds, the bitch pack hunting on Mondays while the dogs' turn came on Thursdays. Even among such a large throng, each hound was known individually by name – names like Harpy, Galloper, Wamba, Carol and Candid. To those responsible for their fitness, "taking the dog for a walk" took on a completely new meaning for, out of season, the hounds were exercised three times a week, *on each day covering an average of 45 miles.* Small wonder, perhaps, that the writer in *The Queen* described them as "the equal of any in the country for work. I have rarely seen a pack in cleaner or harder condition".

Whilst being surprised at the distance covered by the hounds on their exercise runs, I was astonished to hear of Micky, their little terrier friend, who cheerfully accompanied them each mile of the way on every occasion. "Judging from his appearance as well as his performance," said a hunt follower, "Micky's anatomy must have been composed of steel springs".

Then, of course, there were the Hunt horses, splendid creatures with evocative names like York, Shuttlecock, Flash, Hasty Jack, Burnham, Watchit and Warrior. Much of the credit for the condition of both horses and hounds must go to Miss Harker's huntsman, Tom Thackeray, whose story was told in *Echoes of Old Norfolk* and who was never known to miss a single day's hunting – even after a session at the Green Dragon! Then there was the Whip, Wymondham's own George Marshall, covering the miles on Shuttlecock, Watchit or Warrior.

Sybil Harker had her own personal mounts, each almost as distinctive as her, for they were all selected hunters of great merit. Most famous of the string was Donovan, the winner of four firsts at the Royal Show in 1934 and, of course, a big winner locally. Then there was Park Lane, a winner at Richmond Horse Show in 1935, Court Circular, a noted Point-to-Point winner, and St. Patrick. Her favourite mount of all, however, was Saxa, her usual choice when out with the Staghounds.

Sadly and inevitably, however, nothing lasts forever. The years passed and youth gave way to middle age. Then, in 1963, she was saddened by the abolition of deer carting. But she was then in her sixties, and she continued to devote herself to those "good causes". Her face, once aglow with the bloom of youth, took on the signs of having been lived in, though the smile remained to brighten many a day. Then, on November 13th, 1985, having reached the age of 83, her life came to an end.

The local newspaper made great play of the fact that she died a millionaire, a fact which would probably not be considered worthy of mention today, for the world seems suddenly full of such people. She remembered the Red Cross, but her heir was the nearest she ever came to having a son of her own – her nephew, son of the sister for whom, fifty-three years earlier, she had acted as bridesmaid.

The Wymondham Poacher

A crafty old poacher from Wymondham
Caught a sackful of rabbits and skymondham;
    They went in the pot
    And when they were hot
He put them in aspic and tymondham.

Allan Thompson.

November 24th.

I Spy Strangers.

Many of us, filled as we are with an unflagging pride in this county of ours, go blithely through life in the comforting belief that we are "real" Norfolk – Norfolk "through-and-through". After all, we were born here and grew up here, as did our parents, our grandparents and their antecedents. Surely there can be nothing more truly "Norfolk" than that. Yet nothing could be further from the truth, for, in reality, there can be no such thing as a purely Norfolk race of beings. We are, in fact, the product of centuries of hybridisation brought about by the great variety of settlers who, for a variety of reasons, came here and put down new roots in our Norfolk soil.

The incomers who left their mark on our county fell conveniently into two greatly-differing categories – the Invaders and the Strangers. Even the Invaders could also be subdivided, for there can have been no greater contrast than that which existed between the Saxons and the Normans. Saxon history paints a picture of a race of people for whom time was of no great concern. They were persistent, but lethargic. They were not great fighters, but their slow determination gradually engulfed their rivals. In the end, their conquest of our island was little short of a miracle – if, that is, one can apply that word to something which took centuries to complete.

The Normans, on the other hand, were brutally efficient, both in warfare and in the building of stone castles. In such an ancient city as Norwich, the outward signs are typified by the solidity and the sharply-defined lines of the Norman Castle and Cathedral. But, drag yourself away to the parts of the county where rural folk still talk in the manner of their predecessors. There, just listen to the conversation – that's pure Saxon.

Of course, invasions have long been things of the past – 1066 put an end to that. From the beginning of the twelfth century right up to the present day, large numbers of incomers have arrived here, but they have come in peace, often as refugees from religious persecution. The Jews, of course, came for the reasons that have led them to migrate into so many countries. The Flemings came from the Low Countries to help in the expansion of the textile trade, together with the Walloons from the Flemish-speaking areas of Belgium. The Dutch came from the Netherlands as religious and political refugees, whilst from France there came the Huguenot refugees.

It was these various groups of people who became known as the "Strangers" and, lest that should sound a rather cold and unwelcoming title, I would hasten to point out that it was a purely municipal term used by the City authorities, whose duty it was to legislate and provide for the newcomers. This official assistance became of even greater significance when, at one time, the number of Strangers living in Norwich represented a quarter of the total population of the city – 4,000 out of a total of 16,000. Norwich was a city with some degree of national importance at that time, standing side-by-side with London and Canterbury as regards its reputation for providing succour and hospitality to strangers in distress. In spite of present-day accusations to the contrary (largely, I might add, perpetuated by local folk themselves!) Norfolk folk have always been foremost in their welcome to outsiders. Their attitude has always been to "look them up and down" – and then become friends.

Furthermore, it was very much a two-way arrangement, for all those various newcomers left their mark on the city. Much has been written of the Flemish weavers who, up in the garrets of so many of the city's houses, bred canaries to keep them company at their work. Then, while they were producing everything from bombasine to the finest Norwich Lace, others of their kind were bringing fame to another part of the county with their worstead cloth.

Weavers, however, were only part of the story, for there were among them learned lawyers, doctors and men of letters. They became full citizens of Norwich and brought up their offspring as men and women who played a large part in the affairs of the city. The daughters took Norfolk names when they married into the community, but the young men ensured that their European origins would become part of our history. The name of L'Estrange is still there, as also are Beaumont and many more – and we would do well to remember that James and Harriet Martineau are both national figures whom we owe to French-speaking Strangers of Norwich.

Then there were those to whom the land was their métier, in particular the Strangers from the Low Countries. They brought with them their skills and knowledge, and it was not long before Norwich had the reputation of producing the finest fruit and vegetables in the country. It was they who first introduced the idea of cut flowers and, furthermore, it was in 1631 that the first horticultural show in England was held – in Norwich, and organised, needless to say, by the Strangers.

It has always been my belief that Strangers' Hall in Norwich derived its name from its close connection with the immigrants who came here for succour. Standing on the area which we more readily know as Charing Cross, it was originally the Shearers' Cross, a spot where members of the Guild of Sheep-shearers and Cloth-dressers used to meet to conduct their business. We are more familiar with the building as a splendid folk museum – sadly closed as these words are written – but, in my mind, I associate it with those Strangers from Europe, some of whom I always believed to have lived there. Hence my sense of disappointment at reading *If Stones Could Speak*, R.H. Mottram's splendid treatise on the streets and buildings of Norwich, and coming across the following words:

> *What one sees today, used as a very lively and up-to-date Museum, is an accumulation of three or four houses built in different centuries on the same spot. The name "Strangers' Hall" is a mystery; the place had nothing to do with the "strangers" or foreign immigrants into Norwich down the ages, and nothing to do with the L'Estrange family.*

If those words had been written by a more inconsequential writer, I would have dismissed them out of hand, but Ralph Mottram knew his Norwich. I must, therefore, accept his verdict, though I shall always feel a bond of sympathy between the building and the folk who, having received the city's hospitality, repaid it a hundred-fold.

The arrival of European immigrants in this country was, not surprisingly, largely influenced by conditions in their native countries, and the latter years of the 18th century brought a sudden upsurge in numbers as a result of the French Revolution. In spite of the nature of that uprising, however, not all those who sought to flee from the terrors of their country to the peace on our side of the English Channel were aristocrats. Many, in fact, were members of the professional classes who, whilst trying to come to terms with the demands of the revolutionary leaders, found their financial resources being steadily eroded and their working conditions becoming increasingly intolerable.

One such man was the Reverend Thomas d'Eterville, Master of Arts and priest of Caen University. For four years since the start of the revolution he had known that his only hope of survival was to get across that stretch of water and throw himself upon the hospitality of the English, but any hope of achieving that aim was thwarted by the repressive conditions in his homeland. In 1793, however, he knew that he must risk everything in an escape bid, for it was in that year that England declared war on France. He knew that immediate action was imperative if he was to avoid finding himself torn between two warring nations. Hence, he left his home, taking with him his modest life savings, a bag containing a few personal possessions – and just the clothes that he was wearing. On arrival at the port, his feelings of distress became steadily greater, for one rebuff followed another as he tried to find a seaman who would take him across the Channel. Eventually, however, he found a captain who was prepared to risk the dash across that stretch of water – but at the high cost of the wretched refugee's entire life savings as a bribe. Nevertheless, as he stood on the deck and saw the French coast receding, d'Eterville's heart gradually became lighter, for the generosity of the English was well-known. He knew that, when he reached that friendly land, he would be with friends with outstretched arms to greet him. How wrong he was!

He arrived in Dover, dishevelled and penniless, to be greeted with nothing but bleak looks and cold shoulders. His sense of disillusionment was bitter in the extreme, but he was just another in the never-ending line of refugees who had come that way. The people of Dover were heartily sick of down-and-out Frenchies begging for shelter. He soon realised that he had nothing to gain by staying there, and it was then that he decided to set out for Canterbury. As he trod those fifteen miles, though he became steadily more dishevelled and dust-laden, he felt that the influence of the Church would prevail upon the citizens to offer him succour. Once again, however, he was shunned. Perhaps it was his unkempt appearance, suggesting him to be the lowest of vagrants, that caused the inn-keepers of Canterbury to shut their doors in his face. Nevertheless, heartbroken though he was, he was determined not to be beaten. He knew what he would do – he would set his feet out on the weary road to Norwich. And that is exactly what he did, walking all the way!

History does not record how long his journey took, nor, indeed, how he managed to sustain himself on his energy-sapping walk, which, incidentally, left him with a marked stoop that was to stay with him for the rest of his life. Presumably he must have encountered people with a greater sense of compassion than that shown by the citizens of Dover and Canterbury, otherwise he could never have survived such an ordeal. There is, furthermore, no means of knowing why he should have chosen Norwich as his destination, but it seems highly probable that he knew of the large number of his countryfolk who had preceded him and made their home in the city. What we do know is that he found himself among friends who helped him to settle in his adopted county.

He then had to find a way of earning a livelihood, and his only hope in this direction lay in the teaching of French. To this end, on November 24th, he placed an advertisement in the *Norfolk Chronicle,* setting out his terms and qualifications. It cannot be said that the people of Norwich immediately began beating a path to his door but, before long, several of the city schools were calling upon his services. His first pupils were the young ladies of the city's female seminaries, who, it was said, were captivated by his Gallic charm, but his great triumph came when he was invited to join the staff of Norwich Grammar School.

It can truly be said that Fortune smiled upon Thomas d'Eterville on that occasion for, from the mid-sixteenth to the mid-nineteenth century, all the headmasters at that School in the Close had been Classical graduates, who considered the teaching of Classics to be the most important part of their professional lives. It was Edward Valpy, headmaster from 1811 to 1829, who was the first to fall into line with the new school of academic thought that the curriculum should be widened, and it was he who engaged the delighted Frenchman to impart the mysteries of his language to his boarders.

Another of Thomas d'Eterville's pupils at that time was the young George Borrow, who had begged a sum of money from his father to enable him to study not only French, but also Italian and the elements of Spanish. Indeed, the master was enormously impressed by his pupil's exceptional affinity for languages and

Norwich Grammar School as the Reverend Thomas d'Eterville knew it.

foresaw a promising future for him.

By now, the refugee from the French Revolution had become accepted as a true citizen of Norwich, though it must be said that many local people, with that notorious Norfolk inability to come to terms with the pronunciation of foreign names, had sought to simplify matters by shortening his surname in such a way that he became Monsieur De Ville.

It was at this time that he was said to have been living in Strangers' Hall, and he took great delight in walking the city streets wearing the clothes that had survived from his former existence at Caen. These, in the words of a contemporary, consisted of "a snuff-coloured coat, smothered in dust, a pair of drab pantaloons, spotted with grease, and an immense frill of the finest French cambric, which was badly in need of a wash! He was rather tall, of robust build with a remarkable stoop, and a yellowish-red face which blended an expression of bluffness with that of vivacity".

He became steadily more prosperous and, towards the end of his life, he made a will leaving all his money towards furthering the upkeep of Catholic establishments in England. He must have changed his mind before he died, however, for eventually it was a niece and nephew in his native land who received the benefit of

Strangers' Hall, Norwich.

his few hundred pounds of hard-earned Norfolk cash. Yet, who are we to begrudge the last wishes of the man who, having lost everything, started again and happily became one of us?

It is not without a touch of irony that one remembers the arrival in Norwich, a century after Thomas De Ville departed this life, of another group of his compatriots. The year was 1940, and they were Free French soldiers who had fled their homeland in the face of the German Armies' vicious sweep through Europe. They had lived to fight another day.

Once again, Norfolk had "looked them up and down – and then become friends".

Lines By An Exile.

Just let me stay again in that grand county,
Just let me see again the Broadland mists,
Just let me hear those honest Norfolk voices –
Then I can die, and know that Heaven exists.

Jeffrey Sorensen

December 20th.

North Walsham.

A sad news item from the pages of the *Norfolk News* of December 20th, 1862 raises feelings of near-disbelief – and just before Christmas, too!

Selling A Baby.

On Tuesday a circumstance of uncommon occurrence happened in North Walsham – that of a mother selling her child.

A hawker of earthenware called at the house of the mother of the child, one of the beerhouses in the town, soliciting custom for his goods. The woman replied that she did not want to buy anything, but she would sell him the baby "if he liked". The hawker thereupon bought the child for 8d., paid the money, and took the infant away to another house in town.

The circumstance caused much sensation as soon as it became known. Eventually the mother went to reclaim the child, but was refused. She thereupon went to the police station, but could get no redress. Finally, however, an agent was commissioned to effect a re-sale. Half a crown was demanded and paid, and the child restored to its mother again.

Not much remained of the St. Benedict's walls by the time the trams came rumbling past.

A report of a Town Council meeting, from the same issue of the *Norfolk News*, suggests that citizens who flouted planning regulations were treated rather more leniently at that time than are today's transgressors.

The Norwich Walls.

At a meeting of the Norwich Town Council on Tuesday, Mr. Underwood moved that permission be given to Messrs. Buttifant to erect a new shop front to their premises near St. Benedict's Gate, and for that purpose to take down part of the old city wall. Mr. Underwood stated, however, that it would not be necessary to interfere with the old city gates at all.

Mr. A.F. Morgan strongly protested against any such injury to one of the most beautiful relics of Norwich of former times, and there seemed a prospect of a very serious discussion on the subject, when it suddenly came out that the necessary amount of pulling down had already been done, and the question was therefore dismissed with considerable laughter.

187

Christmas.

Glad Tidin's.

This arternune I drawed along ter ar ole village scule;
Tha's savrel year ago since I were there.
An bor, tha's wholly chaanged, that hev - that med me feel a fule;
I felt right lorst at fust, I dew declare.

We hed an inviteertion t'hear the children sing,
An see thar little play - thar "Chris'mas dew".
My Missus, course she come along, she like that sort o' thing;
So we set down a littte arter tew.

As I jus' said, that plaace ha' chaanged; all them long desks ha' gone,
An so's them ole oil lamps what give us light.
They'a got a lot more books an things I couln't maake naathin' on.
They fare as though they're fitted out oright.

Well, sune the boys an gals come in, an then my Missus say,
"John, there's a rea' lot on'em new ter me!"
There's such a crowd o' furriners now live aroun' this way,
Tha's suffin' haard t'know'em all, y'see.

But ar ole neerbour, she set nigh, an bor, she put us right.
She knew thar naames, an where they come from tew.
She's a rea' maaster one, she is – ah, she don't miss a sight;
She know what all the village dew, she dew!

She showed us that there pair o' twins what come from York laast year,
An that there little gal from Wisbech way.
There was three or four from Lunnon, an one from Devonshire,
An even one from Africa, she say.

188

Some others come from Scotland; they're up the faarm, y'see;
Their faather got a tidy bit o' ground.
They don't dew much fer Chris'mas, or so he say t'me,
But New Year's Day he'a asked us t'go round.

Well, I set there, a-thinkin' back. So much come t'my mind
About the paast, an chaanges in ar ways,
An all ar worries, gret an small; I s'pose tha's haard t'find
A lot ter smile about in these here days.

I felt right low . . . then dew yew know, they all began ter sing,
An I looked up, an there them children stood.
An how they sung, newcomers tew! Why, bor, they fared t'bring
Rea' Chris'mas peace an love. That done me good . . .

"Glad tidin's o' gret joy" . . . tha's suffin' we don't orfen hear
When news come in from evrawhere each day.
An yit I b'leeve, at Chris'mas, as another year draw near,
A Little Child can bring that joy ar way . . .

John Kett.

December 31st. New Year's Resolution.

Stop Mobbin'.

Whass the good o'mobbin, bor,
Jest 'cause things look black?
Everywhere 'll be bright an' shinin'
When the sun come back!
Sun in't comin' back? Thass rubbish!
Clouds don't last no while!
They'll pretty soon go chearsin' orf
When they see that yew can smile!

What yew say? Life in't worth livin'?
Blarst, yew mearke me laugh!
Other folk 'as got their troubles –
Some more 'n yew – Not arf!
Wouldn't chearnge my little cottage
With a bloomin' millionaire.
P'raps we can't all hev the grub we want,
But we all can breathe the air!

Hold yew hard, bor; don't talk such squit;
I don't see why yew should.
God mearde the world, an' don't forgit,
He said as it was good.
Thass a really lovely, bew'iful world;
Jest think o' that each minnit.
That in't the world thass wrong, yew know –
Thass jest the people in it!

R.B.

Acknowledgements.

This book owes much to the many old friends who have so willingly shared both memories and photographs with me, and I offer my special thanks to Rhoda Bunn, John Kett, Eddy Riseborough, Mike Softley, Philip Standley, Allan Thompson and Philip Yaxley.

A long overdue word of appreciation also goes to the staff of Wymondham Library and their Norfolk Studies colleagues at Gildengate who, no matter what enquiry is put before them, have the happy knack of unfailingly coming up with the answer.

Bob Bagshaw.
Wymondham.
October 1997.